EDWARD P. LANNING, *the author of this book, has been doing research in Peruvian archaeology since 1956, including excavations at many of the sites discussed in the text. He is Associate Professor of Anthropology at Columbia University and has written numerous articles on the early peoples and civilizations of South America.*

PERU
BEFORE
THE INCAS

Edward P. Lanning

A SPECTRUM BOOK

PRENTICE-HALL, INC., Englewood Cliffs, New Jersey

To EILEEN and MARJORIE

DRAWINGS BY GORDON POLLARD

HINKEY

Preface

Peru is famous as the homeland of the Inca Empire. The Incas, however, were only the last of many prehistoric civilizations in Peru. This book is more concerned with the earlier peoples than with the Incas themselves. Good books and articles about Inca life and government are readily available, and little that is said in them has been changed by subsequent studies. In contrast, recent archaeological studies have dramatically changed our picture of the evolution of the older Peruvian civilizations.

There has been a great explosion in archaeological investigation in Peru since about 1955. Much of the work done since then has not yet seen print, or has been newly printed in esoteric journals and hard-to-find monograph series. I have had the good fortune of participating in the expansion of research, to the extent of four years' field work between 1956 and 1963. During that time, I managed to see most of the still unpublished collections, to visit many of the sites while the work was going on, and to interview some of the researchers at length.

This book has two purposes: to bring together and make public the great mass of new information which has accrued in the last decade, and to offer a theory explaining the growth of prehistoric Peruvian civilization. My aim is to examine the new body of information and to conduct an inquiry into the processes of growth of the ancient civilizations, defining the conditions under which they developed and isolating the factors which contributed to their development. I hope to say not only what the civilizations were, but also why they came into being.

A book of this sort, though signed only by its author, is inevitably the product of many minds. It would be impossible to list all of the persons who have contributed either through giving me information on their research or by discussing archaeological and theoretical problems with me and therefore helping me to clarify my thinking. I can only single out a few persons and institutions and thank them for their contributions to the total effort. For their generosity in letting me use unpublished data, I am especially grateful to Gary Vescelius, Thomas C. Patterson, James Richardson, Rogger Ravinez and Christopher Donnan. The persons who have probably contributed most to the development of the theory presented in this book, either through conversation or through their writings, are John H. Rowe, Thomas C. Patterson, and William Sanders. I would also like to thank Michal D. Coe, Shirley Gorenstein and Lucille G. Lewis, who read and commented on parts of the manuscript, and Gordon R. Willey, who undertook the task of reading and correcting the entire book. My wife, Ruth Eileen, provided not only the patience without which no book is ever finished, but also a fine critique of the theoretical sections. Parts of the book, especially those dealing with the preceramic and early ceramic sequence of the central coast, have been made possible through the support which the Fulbright Commission and the National Science Foundation have given to my research. For the successful completion of the research, I am also indebted for their aid and collaboration to the Museo Nacional de Antropología y Arqueología and the Casa de la Cultura Peruana, and to their directors, Jorge Muelle and Arturo Jiménez Borja. Finally, I want to thank my students, whose interest and penetrating questions have largely shaped the pages which follow.

EDWARD P. LANNING

Contents

I

Introduction

To the Spaniards who discovered the Inca Empire in 1532, it was a source of gold and of souls to be saved. Once they had conquered the Incas, looted the gold, and converted the Indians to Christianity, the native population became a source of cheap labor in mines, fields and textile mills. It is only in the last century, with the rise of a new consciousness of—and perhaps a new conscience about—the American past, that the sciences of ethnohistory and archaeology have turned to the serious study of the ancient people of Peru.

In 1946 the Institute of Andean Research sponsored an intensive study of the archaeology of the Virú Valley on the north coast of Peru. This study, which revolutionized Peruvian archaeology in various ways, also had a noteworthy effect on books about prehistoric Peru. For several years the Virú Valley was the only part of Peru whose entire culture history back to 2500 B.C. had been studied. A number of books have relied on the results of the Virú Valley project for their organization.[1] Quite naturally, each of them

---

[1] Wendell C. Bennett and Junius B. Bird, *Andean Culture History,* Handbook Series No. 15 (New York: American Museum of Natural History, 1949); G. H. S. Bushnell, *Peru,* Ancient Peoples and Places (London: Thames and Hudson, 1956); J. Alden Mason, *The Ancient Civilizations of Peru,* Pelican Books A395 (Harmondsworth, Middlesex: Penguin Books Ltd., 1957).

has tended to interpret the whole of Peruvian prehistory on the basis of the sequence of events in the Virú Valley. Their authors were looking into the mansion of Peru through the keyhole of one tiny north coastal valley, for the simple reason that they had no other vantage point available.

Subsequent research may not have opened the door, but it has certainly multiplied the number of keyholes through which we can look. Whereas the Virú sequence extends back to 2500 B.C., the central coast and the central highlands have now been studied on much earlier time levels. The archaeological sequences of a number of coastal valleys are now better known than is that of Virú. Recent studies in the highlands have made it apparent that we cannot automatically apply conclusions drawn from the coast to the whole of ancient Peru. New research has produced not only new facts, but also new relationships between facts. Simple developmental schemes based on the Virú sequence are no longer adequate to describe the course of Peruvian cultural evolution. Archaeologists are seeking new concepts to explain the rise of the ancient Andean civilizations.

An inquiry into the nature and causes of ancient civilizations is best begun by saying what is meant by the word "civilization." In general, when we say that such-and-such a people were civilized, we mean that they were organized in a large, complicated society with a government, centered in a specific capital, which controlled the destinies of a large population. Civilization, in this sense, is contrasted to the "tribal" society of nomadic hunters and gatherers or of farmers or fishermen living in largely independent villages.

The only way to define civilization is to look at all of the ancient and modern societies that are generally considered to be "civilized," and to find out what characteristics they have in common. Archaeologists working in Europe and the Near East have tended to stress metallurgy, writing and monumental architecture as the identifying marks of civilization, probably because all three are easy to identify in the archaeological record. When we look at the ancient American civilizations, however, we find that these criteria are not universally valid. The ancient Peruvians built their great civilizations without any knowledge whatsoever of writing, and the classic Maya civilization of southern Mexico, Guatemala, and British Honduras knew nothing of metal working.

Monumental architecture is still a good criterion of civilization, but it is not enough by itself. The essence of civilization is its type of organization, not its material manifestations. All civilizations, both ancient and modern, in the New World or Old, have had the following characteristics:

1. Subsistence based on intensive agriculture, with or without animal husbandry.
2. Relatively large, dense populations.
3. Efficient systems for the distribution of foodstuffs, raw materials, and luxury goods over fairly large areas.
4. A diversity of settlement types, including either cities or ceremonial centers as the focus of sociopolitical organization.
5. State structures, with central governments exerting varying degrees of control over the lives of people in many settlements.
6. Intensive social stratification.
7. Extensive occupational specialization in which only a part of the population is involved in the production of food, while the remainder are craftsmen, administrators, merchants, and so forth.

There are many cases of uncivilized societies which have developed one or another of these characteristics, especially social stratification, occupational specialization and efficient distributive systems. No "tribal" society, however, shows more than two or three of these patterns, whereas all seven of them are characteristic of all civilizations.

A civilization, like any other way of life, is an adaptive mechanism that serves to insure the survival and prosperity of a human population. The great success of civilization, which has spread around the world at the expense of other modes of life, is due to its adaptive efficiency. Unlike other socioeconomic systems, civilization is capable of supporting and organizing very large populations and of overcoming the barriers of vastly different physical environments. An inquiry into the causes of civilization, then, is also an inquiry into the reasons for man's spectacular success in dominating our planet.

Briefly, the culture history of Peru is one of economic and social adaptation to a land of climatic and topographic extremes. Efficient exploitation of locally rich resources, especially for farming, herding, and fishing, led to rapid growth of population. At the same time, habitable regions were of limited size and were separated from each other by arid deserts or great mountain masses. The expanding population was thus densely concentrated in small zones which were semi-isolated from each other. The expansion of limited farming and grazing lands could only be carried out efficiently on a valley-wide or regional basis. Local states provided the social cohesion and control necessary to such undertakings.

Much of Peruvian culture history was colored by the conflict between the expansive tendencies of these states and the isolative nature of the environment. This conflict is reflected in alternating periods of regional diversity and interregional unification. During the latter periods, the spread of cults or the expansion of empires opened up lines of trade and communication. The flow of goods and ideas inspired innovation and promoted rapid, basic cultural change. For example, the earliest of the great cities of northern Peru were built as a result of southern influence during such a period of unification. Bronze made its appearance during a period of unification, and bronze tools became abundant and widespread during another such period.

The regional cultures were never submerged, but they were profoundly altered by these innovations. The intervening periods of regional isolation reflect the difficulty of holding together such a diverse and broken-up country. During these periods the widespread innovations were reworked and integrated into new patterns as the regional cultures crystallized into new forms. This process, in turn, provided a fund of cultural variety to be spread during the next period of unification.

Many other factors entered into this process. Most of them probably remain to be discovered, but some are known. During the earlier part of the Preceramic Stage, for example, an ongoing process of desiccation gradually prevented man from exploiting large areas of the coast (see Chapter IV). The drying-out reached its peak about 2500 B.C., thereafter encouraging habitation in the more productive zones of shore and river valley.

The geographic differences between the coast and the highlands must have played a fundamental role in the growth of civilization. Apart from their different crops, construction techniques, and opportunities for communication, they had different configurations of population distribution. The coastal valleys are small and were densely populated. They could support their inhabitants only with the aid of extensive, valley-wide irrigation systems. In short, the coastal civilizations were classic examples of "hydraulic societies," in which the state structure responded to the need for control of water resources.

In the highlands, on the other hand, rainfall agriculture was feasible, and irrigation and terracing played a fairly minor role in augmenting the fertility of the land. There are several great highlands river basins which provided open communications over considerable distance. As a result, more separated population centers became the foci of competing local and regional states. The major movements of interregional unification originated in these highlands basins, usually when one of the local states succeeded in expanding through conquest. Although the small coastal states also competed for dominance, none of them ever conquered the highlands. Rather, they fell repeatedly before armies and ideologies coming out of the highlands area.

II

The Country

The word "Peru" is generally used by archaeologists to include not only the modern Republic of Peru, but also the highlands of Bolivia and often the northernmost part of Chile as well. This area is located on the western side of South America, extending from just south of the Equator to about 20° south latitude. The countryside is dominated by the great mountain mass of the Central Andes, which makes up more than half of the area. To the west, the Pacific Ocean has always been a major factor in the life of the people.

Because of its nearness to the Equator, its great altitudes, and its association with the ocean, Peru is a country of geographic extremes. Its climates range from some of the most idyllic to among the most extreme conditions under which mankind has lived anywhere in the world. Traveling only a few hundred miles from west to east, one may pass through the driest desert, well-watered upland valleys, intensely cold high peaks and plateaus, and on to the rank and stifling tropical rain forest. To the west, water and wood are precious commodities; to the east, great rivers meander through lush forests. The man who lives at sea level cannot change places with the man who lives at an altitude of 15,000 feet without both of them going through an extended and painful period of acclimatization. While sand dunes slowly cover houses and fields on the coast, torrential rains bring on landslides that destroy whole villages in the highlands.

Such extremes of living conditions have necessarily had a profound effect on the lives of the people. In part, the history of ancient Peruvian culture is the history of man's successful efforts to adapt himself to these varied climates and topographies and—with the exception of the low tropical forest—to dominate the region as a whole. Great irrigation and terracing projects led to corn fields in the desert and on the steepest mountain slopes. An extensive road system carried the produce of farm and sea across one of the world's highest mountain ranges. Through the centuries, cults and technologies spread from highlands to low and from lowlands to high, regardless of barriers, and eventually the Inca armies proved superior, not only to their enemies, but also to all of the exigencies of climate and terrain.

THE OCEAN

Much of Peruvian archaeology becomes meaningful only when we understand the role of the Pacific Ocean, both as a source of food and as a controller of climate. Thanks to its cold current, it is unusually rich in edible life. It is also the sole cause of the extreme aridity that has always conditioned life on the Peruvian coast.

The prevalent southeasterly winds that blow along the coast hustle the surface waters away from the shore, creating an upwelling of cold water from the ocean depths to replace them. Oceanographers call this upwelling current the *Peru Coastal Current*. Popularly it is known as the *Humboldt Current*. It brings up nutrients from the ocean bottom and leads to the rich growth of plankton, providing a constantly renewed source of food for the larger forms of marine life, which therefore abound. In ancient times, fish were caught with hooks and lines and with a variety of nets, which were manipulated either from the beach or by men mounted on inflated skins or small rafts made of bundles of rushes.

Not only were the larger fishes numerous and easily caught, but the smaller ones—schools of anchovies—were important to agriculture as the ultimate source of fertilizer. They may have been used directly as such, as they sometimes are today. However, the anchovies provided food for the countless flocks of cormorants, gulls, and pelicans which in turn deposited the thick layers of guano used anciently as fertilizer (and exhaustively mined during the last century and a half). These shore birds, too, were an important source of food on the coast in ancient times, as were sea lions, dogfish, and rays. Shellfish, principally mussels and clams, were also abundant in many places along the coast.

The cold waters of the Peru Coastal Current cool the air over the ocean so that evaporation is held to a minimum. As the cool air moves in over the land, it is constantly warmed. The warming, together with a low temperature gradient, increases the air's capacity to hold its evaporated water, effectively preventing rainfall on the coast and at the same time providing cool weather in spite of the tropical latitude. As a result, the coastal plain is an absolutely dry, yet cool, desert, while the air is usually humid. In fact, six to eight winter months of overcast skies and frequent dense fogs are the rule over much of the Peruvian coast.

At its northern end the cold current is diverted around the Gulf of Guayaquil, on the Peru-Ecuador border, by the westward bulge of the continent. It strikes the Ecuadorean coast to the north of the Gulf, then swings westward before reaching Manta on the central coast of Ecuador. From Manta northward and in the Gulf of Guayaquil it is replaced by warm currents. In these areas the coastal desert gives way to lush tropical forests and mangrove swamps. The southern coast of Ecuador, between Manta and the Gulf, is a cool desert which differs from that of Peru in that it gets a little rain each year, though not enough to permit farming.

Occasionally the upwelling current fails and warm waters move in from the north, some brought by the Equatorial Countercurrent, others flowing out of the Gulf of Guayaquil. Both of these warm currents are called the *Niño*. The change in water temperature is reflected by rainfall in far northern Peru, increased rain in the highlands, scarcity of anchovies, and the death by starvation of great numbers of guano birds along most of the coast. Only rarely—not since 1925—is the effect of this change so intense as to produce much rain as far south as the central coast of Peru.

THE LAND

The Andes, running from northwest to southeast, divide Peru into three long, narrow topographic and climatic zones: the desert coast, including the western slope of the mountains; the highlands; and the *montaña* or tropical forest on the eastern slope of the mountains. The coastal plain is a long narrow flatland, traversed in an east-west direction by Andean outliers and by some forty small rivers. These rivers have their headwaters in the western range of the Andes, and only one of them is fed by one of the intermontane highlands rivers. This exception is the Santa, which in its upper portion passes through a highlands valley known as the *Callejón de Huaylas*.

The entire coast, except for the northernmost tip of Peru on the Gulf of Guayaquil, is one of the world's driest deserts. Except for mist from the fogs that cover much of the terrain in wintertime, there is almost never any measurable rain. Nevertheless, the coastal plain is anything but a wasteland. The river valleys, which were originally wooded, are irrigated and intensely farmed. Cotton and sugar are the principal crops today; cotton and maize were probably the most important of the ancient crops. The rivers run full only from December to March—the summer rainy season in the highlands. The smaller of them run dry during the winter, but the larger ones have some water all year round. In their upper courses, the rivers run through narrow gorges, while the lower parts of the valleys spread out in delta formation. The flow in the lower valleys has been considerably reduced during the last 2000 years by the extraction of water for irrigation. Before that, the larger rivers probably flooded parts of their valleys every year, renewing the soil with new layers of silt.

Most of the inter-valley areas consist of barren hills or sand flats, and sand dunes are actively building in many places. Here and there are patches of *Tillandsia*, a bromelia that takes its minimal water from the air rather than from the soil. On the southern and far northern portions of the coast, especially around Ica and Piura, the water table is high enough to permit the growth of clumps of mesquites. In areas of dense winter fogs, grasses, bushes and other plants manage to thrive on trapped and condensed moisture. Such areas of fog vegetation are known as *lomas*. They have a relatively rich fauna of foxes, lizards, birds, and snails, and one occasionally sees a deer or guanaco (a wild relative of the llama) which has come down out of the highlands to graze. Both the *lomas* and the mesquites were formerly much more extensive than at present (see pp. 48 and 55).

Well up on the slopes of the mountains, varying in altitude from 5500 feet in the south to about 1500 feet in the north, cacti and a few bushes make their appearance. In the farthest north this formation gives way to tropical grasslands and woods which, at Tumbes on the southern edge of the Gulf of Guayaquil, reach down to the sea.

The highlands are a fairly young mountain mass, high and rugged. They are traversed by several major rivers which, running north-south, divide the mountains into parallel chains. Where there are three such ranges, they are known as the *Cordillera Occidental, Central,* and *Oriental,* while the ranges flanking the Callejón de Huaylas bear the names of *Cordillera Blanca* and *Cordillera Negra.* The principal rivers dissecting the highlands are the Marañon, Huallaga, upper Santa, Mantaro, Apurimac and Urubamba. The Ucayali borders the highlands on the east. Between Peru and Bolivia lies Lake Titicaca, the highest major body of water in the world. Some of the smaller valleys contain lakes impounded by ancient glacial deposits, and some very high valleys are still filled by glaciers.

Though the smaller valleys were and are farmed, the areas of primary importance to man have always been the large basins and the high plateaus. With the aid of irrigation and terracing, both the valley bottoms and the surrounding slopes were cultivated. The highest of the cultivated basins is the plateau area around Lake Titicaca, the *altiplano.* The highest plateaus, known as *punas,* are inhabited to altitudes of 15,000 feet and higher. They are covered with low grasses and bushes, and serve primarily as pasture for flocks of llamas and alpacas. They were once the favorite summer haunts of the hunting peoples who lived in the highlands during the Preceramic Stage.

Summer, from December to March, is the rainy season in the highlands. Additional water is provided in April and May by the melting of the snows on the higher slopes. Although the life of the country depends on the mountain rains, they are not always beneficial. They lead to frequent landslides which, either directly or by causing the overflow of impounded lakes, block roads and bury houses or occasionally whole villages.

Active volcanos, with their attendant earthquakes, are found only in the southern part of the highlands.

The eastern jungle area can be considered as divided into two areas, *selva* and *montaña*. The *selva,* at the foot of the mountains, is Amazonia: typical South American tropical rain forest, traversed by broad, slow meandering rivers and streams which frequently change course, covered by a great variety of trees of which the most important, economically, is the rubber tree. It was and is the home of "wild" Indians who live by slash-and-burn farming and by hunting and fishing.

The *montaña* is geographically and culturally a zone of transition. It is wet and heavily forested, and its upper portion is shrouded in mist. Because of the combination of intense rains and steep mountain sides, the high cloud forest is a dangerous area which may not have been much exploited either for agriculture or as pasture. Nevertheless, several important archaeological sites are located in both the high and low *montaña.*

To the north and south of the Central Andes the countryside changes. The Ecuadorean coast is not so favorable for human occupation as the Peruvian coast. Around the Gulf of Guayaquil, from Tumbes to Posorja, it is lined with mangrove swamps and covered with tropical rain forest. From Posorja north to Manta, the southern coast of Ecuador is a cool desert, whose average rainfall of two inches a year makes it slightly rainier than the desert of Peru, but incapable of supporting rainfall agriculture and largely lacking the rivers that make irrigation farming possible in Peru. North of Manta the mangroves reappear and the forest again reaches the coast. The northern coast of Ecuador and the entire

Pacific coast of Colombia and Panama are infamous for the impenetrability of their swamps and jungles. The southern Ecuadorean desert is a quite recent phenomenon, however. Until 1500 or 1000 B.C. the mangroves extended continuously across the whole coast from the Gulf to Manta, and about 5000 B.C. they seem to have reached as far south as Talara.

Southern Ecuador has another geographical feature that is lacking in Peru. Inland from the desert coast and separated from it by a coastal range, the Guayas Basin provides a large, fertile tropical valley which is now largely under cultivation. This basin has been a major population center during the last 3000 years. The Ecuadorean highlands are much like their Peruvian counterpart, but the major river valleys are not so large and are separated from each other by mountain massifs of staggering proportions.

To the south of the Central Andes, the desert extends along the entire northern half of Chile, but soon changes character. A large area of interior drainage, comparable to the Basin-and-Range Province of North America, takes up much of northern Chile, western Bolivia, and northwestern Argentina. Here the desert is at its widest, extending far up into the highlands. Except in very rare years (1925 and 1953 are the most recent) there is no rainfall except at the highest altitudes—above 11,000 feet on the Chilean side. This area of interior drainage includes the Atacama Desert and the Pampa de Tamarugal in Chile, the Puna de Jujuy in Argentina, and the *salares* of Bolivia. The rivers here are derived largely from scant rainfall on the high mountains, partly from the overflow of Lake Titicaca. They drain into a series of salt lakes where the water evaporates or sinks into the sand. Only one river on the Chilean side, the Río Loa, holds its water and drains into the Pacific Ocean. South of Camarones—the last of the Peru-type coastal valleys—the coast is craggy and utterly barren, though it was occupied anciently by enterprising fishermen.

THE PEOPLE

The Indians of ancient Peru, like their modern descendants, were short and stocky, with short, medium to broad heads, relatively short faces, and noses of moderate breadth. The highlands

Indians had slightly narrower heads than those of the coast. To-day's Indians—who comprise half the population of Peru—have brown or coppery skins, dark eyes and straight black hair. The internal epicanthic fold, which produces the oriental "slant" eye, is well developed. Like most American Indians, a high proportion of Peruvian Indians have blood of type O.

The Indians of the highlands show a series of special adaptations to the altitude—adaptations which must surely have been present in their prehistoric ancestors as well. Their deep barrel chests result from their unusually large lungs. Not only do they have more blood, but they also have a higher count of red corpuscles and therefore more hemoglobin, which of course leads to a more efficient and rapid distribution of oxygen to the body tissues. This increase in the quantity of hemoglobin is apparently not an inherited characteristic, since Indians who move down to the coast become acclimatized through the reduction of their red corpuscles, while non-Indians who move to the highlands undergo a gradual increase in the oxygen-carrying capacity of their blood.

As a result of these physiological adaptations, the highlands Indians are not inconvenienced by the rarified air of the altitudes at which they live. If properly nourished, a highlands Indian is no more fatigued by a day's hard work than is a lowlander. On holidays they take part in vigorous dances for hours at a time, unaffected by the scarcity of oxygen in their mountain atmosphere.

The ancient Peruvians often modified their skulls for esthetic or surgical reasons. In many regions infants' heads were deformed by applying pressure with boards and straps, so that the individual would grow up with a head that was excessively long, perfectly round, or short and high, according to the local standards of beauty. Trephining—the surgical removal of a piece of the skull by cutting, scraping, or drilling—was widely practiced, especially in the highlands. It has been estimated that somewhat over 60 per cent of the patients survived the operation. In one case, the cut-out bone was replaced by a gold plate.

When the Incas conquered Peru, the country was divided into a great number of small groups, each speaking its own language. The new emperors imposed the Inca language (usually called *Quechua*) to facilitate trade and administration. Subsequently the

Spanish, rather than learn such a variety of local languages, not only fostered the speaking of *Quechua* but even taught it in some regions that the Incas had never reached. It is spoken today by nearly half of the ten million inhabitants of the Republic of Peru.

The second most important language, and the only one other than *Quechua* spoken by a large number of people today, is *Aymara.* It is and was spoken through much of the Bolivian highlands and on the Peruvian side of Lake Titicaca. It may have had a wider distribution in southern Peru before being replaced by *Quechua* during Inca and post-Inca times. On the other hand, the Inca emperors were responsible for some degree of spread of the *Aymara* language, since they transferred colonies of *Aymara* speakers from their homeland to other regions such as Arequipa.

Most of the ancient Peruvian languages have been lost. Their vocabularies and grammars were not recorded, and in many cases we do not even know their names. The ancient coastal languages are entirely extinct, and the only other highlands languages spoken by a few survivors are *Uru* and *Chipaya,* around Lakes Titicaca and Poopó. Only in the lower *montaña* and the *selva,* among peoples who were not conquered by the Incas nor, effectively, by the Spanish, is the ancient linguistic diversity still found. Many of these jungle languages have been studied, but many more—some of which may also soon disappear—are little known.

PLANTS AND ANIMALS

Most of the plants grown by the ancient Peruvians were indigenous to the area. A few came from the tropical lowlands of South America, some apparently from Mexico or Central America. Potatoes, maize, and cotton were perhaps the most important for the area as a whole, but there was considerable variety according to altitude and growing conditions. Table 1 lists the more important plants grown in ancient Peru. In addition to those given in the table, many wild plants were gathered as food, and a great many plants were grown or gathered for the manufacture of dyes, cordage, and wooden objects, and for medicinal purposes.

Different plants were grown at different altitudes. In the highest mountain valleys were grown potatoes, *quinoa, cañihua, oca,*

TABLE 1

Major Cultivated Plants of Ancient Peru

Crop Type	Common Name	Botanical Name
GRAINS	Maize	*Zea mays*
	Quinoa	*Chenopodium quinoa*
	Cañihua	*Chenopodium pallidicaula*
	Amaranth	*Amaranthus caudatus*
	"	*Amaranthus cruentus*
LEGUMES	Common bean	*Phaseolus vulgaris*
	Lima bean	*Phaseolus lunatus*
	Jack bean	*Canavalia* sp.
	Tarwi	*Lupinus* sp.
	Peanut	*Arachis hypogaea*
CUCURBITS	Squash	*Cucurbita maxima*
	"	*Cucurbita moschata*
	"	*Cucurbita ficifolia*
	Gourd	*Lagenaria siceraria*
ROOTS	Potato	*Solanum* sp.
	Oca	*Oxalis tuberosa*
	Ulluco	*Ullucus tuberosus*
	Añu	*Tropaeolum tuberosum*
	Achira	*Canna edulis*
	"	*Canna indica*
	Jíquima	*Pachyrhizus* sp.
	Arracacha	*Arracacia xanthorrhiza*
	Manioc	*Manihot esculenta*
	Sweet potato	*Ipomoea batatas*
FRUITS	Pineapple	*Ananas comosus*
	Guanábana, soursop	*Annona muricata*
	Chirimoya	*Annona cherimola*
	Avocado	*Persea americana*
	Pacae	*Inga* sp.
	Guava	*Psidium guajava*
	Lúcuma	*Lucuma bifera*
	Pepino	*Solanum muricatum*
	Molle	*Schinus molle*
	Ciruela del fraile	*Bunchosia armeniaca*
OTHERS	Cotton	*Gossypium barbadense*
	Chili pepper, ají	*Capsicum* sp.
	Coca	*Erythroxylon coca*
	Tobacco	*Nicotiana tabacum*
	"	*Nicotiana rustica*

ulluco, and *añu.* The same plants grew in the lower highlands valleys along with maize, *tarwi, molle,* squash, chili peppers, amaranth, *pacae,* and *lúcuma.* The coastal valleys produced maize, beans, peanuts, squash, gourds, manioc, sweet potato, *achira, jíquima,* pineapple, *guanábana, chirimoya,* guava, avocado, *pacae, lúcuma, pepino,* cotton, and chili peppers. Plants of special importance in the *montaña* were maize, manioc, coca and tobacco.

Most of these plants were originally domesticated in the Andes, and many of them were never cultivated elsewhere in America. One group, however, seems to have had its origin to the north, probably in Mexico. This group includes maize, squash (at least *Cucurbita moschata*), gourds, common beans, jack beans, avocados, chili peppers, and amaranth. Both maize and squash were introduced into Peru at a very early date and went through a long process of local selection and hybridization, so that Peruvian varieties were not the same as those being grown in Mexico. Manioc and peanuts were almost certainly first cultivated in the tropical lowlands of South America, whence they spread to Peru. On the other hand, some plants that spread widely through ancient America, such as tobacco, the sweet potato and the lima bean, were probably first cultivated in Peru. The history of cultivated cotton is still obscure, but it may have been at least as old in Peru as in Mexico. Some plants that did not spread beyond the Andes in ancient times were nevertheless taken up by the Spaniards and introduced first into Europe, thence to the rest of the world. The potato, so familiar on our dinner tables, is the most noteworthy of the ancient Peruvian contributions to the diet of the modern world.

Both wild and domesticated animals played their role in the life of the ancient Andean people. The food animals of the ocean and shore have already been mentioned. The fauna of the coastal desert is meager; the animals most frequently met here are lizards, foxes, and field owls. In the highlands live the guanaco and vicuña (the wild camelids; see p. 17), the Andean deer, the puma, and the *viscacha* (a large edible rodent). As one travels down the *montaña,* one may meet jaguars, peccaries, tapirs, monkeys, boas, and, in fact, the whole varied fauna of the tropical rain forest.

Domestic animals were more varied and more important in the

Andes than anywhere else in ancient America. They included the dog and the muscovy duck, both of which were widespread beyond the Andes, and the llama, the alpaca, and the cavy or guinea pig. The dog, of course, was man's companion as it is everywhere in the world. The Inca dog was a medium-sized breed, short-haired and short-legged. It served as a pet and scavenger, and was used for hunting by some of the pre-Inca peoples. The muscovy (*Cairina moschata*) is a large duck which was raised for its meat.

The most important animals, both wild and domestic, were the American camelids, the llama (*Lama glama glama*), the guanaco (*Lama glama guanicoe*), the alpaca (*Lama pacos*), and the vicuña (*Lama vicugna* or *Vicugna vicugna*). The llama and alpaca are and were domesticated; the guanaco and vicuña exist only in a wild state. The guanaco is usually considered to represent the wild ancestor of the llama.

Alpacas were raised almost exclusively for their wool. Llamas provided wool of a somewhat inferior grade, and were used as pack animals and occasionally as sources of meat. Both species were used as sacrifices in religious ceremonies. Though it is often affirmed that these animals bred well only in the highlands, there is no good evidence to this effect. Small herds are successfully bred on the coast today. Certainly the large numbers of their bones found in coastal midden sites, and the extensive use of their wool on the coast even at periods when there is no evidence of trade with the highlands, imply that considerable herds were raised on the coast in ancient times. The rarity of llamas on the coast today is due to competition with animals introduced by the Spanish. The donkey carries bigger loads than the llama, and coastal Peruvians prefer beef on their tables and sheep's wool in their clothing.

Guanacos lived throughout the central and southern highlands and, in larger numbers, in Argentina and Chile. The habitat of the vicuña is the high *puna*. Both wild forms were hunted in ancient times, the guanaco primarily for its meat, the vicuña for its fine wool.

Cavies were raised throughout the Central Andes as a source of meat. They were kept in the houses and fed table scraps and fodder. Though a single cavy does not have much meat, their high fertility rate and the ease of raising them made them worth while as food animals. The Indians of the highlands still raise and eat cavies, and they are considered a delicacy by the non-Indians of the coast. If we had any way of estimating the number of guinea pigs eaten in ancient times, we might find that they ranked with seafood as the most important sources of protein in the ancient diet, well ahead of the camelids and the Andean deer.

III

The Archaeological
Background

The Spaniards who discovered Peru early in the sixteenth century were struck not only by the organization and complexity of Inca civilization, but also by the grandeur and wealth of the ruins in Inca territory. In a sense, Peruvian archaeology goes back to Pedro Cieza de Leon, a Spanish soldier who recorded his observations on ruins and other antiquities in 1553. Interest in Peruvian antiquities has continued high ever since. For centuries, though, the antiquities were treated as curiosities, as treasures, or as art objects. It was not until the latter part of the nineteenth century that the new science of archaeology brought in the idea of studying ancient monuments as a way of reconstructing culture history.

Beginning with Ephraim George Squier's excavations at Pachacamac in 1864, a number of archaeologists and explorers carried on surveys and excavations of archaeological sites in Peru. The outstanding names of the late nineteenth century are well known to students of Peruvian prehistory: Thomas J. Hutchinson, Wilhelm Reiss, Alphons Stübel, Charles Wiener, E. W. Middendorf, Adolph Bandelier. These pioneers were not yet conducting scientific research in the modern sense. They had little interest in chronology. They did not employ stratigraphic techniques in excavation, nor did they make much use of archaeological associations. They concentrated their attention on the reconstruction of the ancient cultures that they were studying, but not on the history of those cultures.

The era of modern archaeology was initiated by the great German archaeologist, Max Uhle. Uhle introduced the techniques of stratigraphy in his excavation at Pachacamac in 1896. His report, published in 1903, was the first example of true archaeological stratigraphy in the Americas.[1] From 1899 to 1909 Uhle excavated extensively in cemeteries all along the Peruvian coast, defining many of the ancient cultures that are now among the most famous in American prehistory. Comparing these cultures with the stratigraphic sequence at Pachacamac, he evolved a scheme of four major periods (pre-Tiahuanaco, Tiahuanaco, post-Tiahuanaco, and Inca) for all of Peru. This chronological system is still the basis of all significant interpretations of Peruvian prehistory, though it has been greatly refined and extended much further back into the past.

As it happens, Uhle never published the evidence for his conclusions. They were thus not generally accepted by archaeologists until the mid-1920's, when Alfred L. Kroeber, William Duncan Strong, and Anna H. Gayton studied Uhle's collections and published a series of classic monographs that established Uhle's chronological system beyond cavil.

The most prominent field investigators of the 1920's and 1930's were Kroeber, Wendell C. Bennett, and Julio C. Tello. Among them, they explored and excavated in many parts of Peru, discovering new cultures and throwing new light on those cultures that had been defined by Uhle's work. Of first importance, perhaps, was Tello's formulation of what he called the "Chavín Culture"— actually a widespread cult and art style which linked up many local cultures on a time level earlier than Uhle's "Pre-Tiahuanaco."

Still another step back into the past was taken in 1941-42. At that time the Institute for Andean Research organized a series of

[1] Max Uhle, *Pachacamac: Report of the William Pepper, M.D., LL.D., Peruvian Expedition of 1896* (Philadelphia: University of Pennsylvania, 1903).

expeditions to various parts of the country. One of the excavations of the central coast expedition, made by Gordon R. Willey and Marshall T. Newman, was in an early shellheap which Uhle had discovered at Ancón. Here the excavators discovered the first specimens of pottery earlier than the Chavín style, belonging to the period which we now call the Initial Period. This excavation also produced the first evidence of chronological change within these very early pottery periods.

In 1946 the Institute for Andean Research again sent a number of archaeologists to Peru, this time to concentrate their efforts in the Virú Valley on the north coast. This project had many important results. It led to the discovery and excavation of the first preceramic sites identified in Peru. It was the first time that an entire valley had been systematically surveyed with the intention of working out its total culture history. It led, a few years later, to the determination of the first radiocarbon dates for Peru. Probably its most important result, however, was the publication of Gordon Willey's history of settlement patterns in the Virú Valley.[2] This book changed the course of investigation of Peruvian prehistory. Before the Virú Valley Project, Peruvian archaeology had consisted largely of the working out of ceramic chronologies and the excavation of a few selected ruins. Willey traced the history of the human settlements in the Virú Valley, relating them to their geographical environment, population growth, warfare, relationships with neighboring valleys, agricultural needs and the development of irrigation systems, and other historical and environmental phenomena. In other words, he attempted a study of the total culture history of the valley within its total environmental setting. This holistic approach has characterized much of subsequent research in Peru and has given us many important insights into the nature and causes of the growth of ancient Peruvian civilization.

Since the conclusion of the Virú Valley Project, and especially since about 1955, there has been a great deal more archaeological research in Peru than ever before. A list of the participating institutions would be practically a catalog of the major universities and

[2] Gordon R. Willey, *Prehistoric Settlement Patterns in the Virú Valley, Peru*, Bureau of American Ethnology, Bulletin 155 (Washington, D.C.: Smithsonian Institution, 1953).

museums of the United States, western and central Europe, and Peru, and would include also such institutions as the University of Tokyo and the Museo de La Plata in Argentina. Chronologies have been amended and vastly refined. New cultures have been discovered almost yearly. The time span of human occupation has been pushed back many thousands of years further into the past. A beginning has been made on the task of relating the processes of cultural change to changes in climate and topography, demography, and ancient political and military events. Archaeologists have penetrated the jungles of the *montaña* for the first time, and have extended their studies northward and southward to the limits of the Central Andes both on the coast and in the highlands. In short, we now know many times more about ancient Peru than we did when the archaeologists of the Virú Valley Project went there in 1946.

STAGES AND PERIODS

The Virú Valley Project led to three books and several articles which attempted to bring together a large amount of new information in an organized fashion. The authors of these papers organized their material into categories known to archaeologists as *developmental stages,* that is, successive units of cultural development that were felt to be applicable over the whole of the Central Andes. For example, W. D. Strong divided Peruvian prehistory into successive stages labeled Pre-agricultural, Developmental, Formative, Florescent, Fusion and Imperial.[3] For Julian Steward, the stages were Pre-agricultural, Basic Agricultural Beginnings, Basic Inter-areal Developmental (or Formative), Regional Formative (or Developmental), Regional Florescent, and Empire and Conquest.[4] Wendell C. Bennett called the stages Early Farmers, Cultist, Ex-

[3] William Duncan Strong, "Cultural Epochs and Refuse Stratigraphy in Peruvian Archaeology," in *A Reappraisal of Peruvian Archaeology*, ed. Wendell C. Bennett, Memoir No. 4 (Menasha, Wis.: Society for American Archaeology, 1948), pp. 93-102.

[4] Julian H. Steward, "A Functional-Developmental Classification of American High Cultures," in *A Reappraisal of Peruvian Archaeology*, ed. Wendell C. Bennett, Memoir No. 4 (Menasha, Wis.: Society for American Archaeology, 1948), pp. 103-4.

perimenter, Mastercraftsman, Expansionist, City Builder, and Imperialist.[5] G. H. S. Bushnell used the same scheme in 1956, but added an "Early Hunters" stage and renamed Mastercraftsman "classic." [6] J. Alden Mason, in *The Ancient Civilizations of Peru,* combined Strong's and Bennett's systems, naming his stages Pre-Agricultural, Early Agricultural, Developmental (including, successively, Formative, Cultist, and Experimental), Florescent, and Climactic (including Expansionist, Urbanist, and Imperialist).[7]

Unfortunately, the use of these developmental stage designations has introduced more confusion than clarity into Peruvian archaeology. There are both practical and theoretical reasons for this. To begin with, the application of such terms as "Formative" and "Classic" is entirely subjective. Bushnell, for example, defined the "Classic" as marked "not only by the full development of technical processes . . . and by flourishing art styles, but by the establishment of highly organized and aggressive states." [8] He included in it some of the cultures belonging to the Early Intermediate Period (200 B.C. to A.D. 600). Bennett placed the same cultures in his Mastercraftsman stage. Yet few archaeologists who have worked in Cuzco or on the central coast would agree that the local cultures of this period deserve either name, whether by Bushnell's and Bennett's definitions or by any other. For me, at least, the "classic" culture of Cuzco was that of the Incas of the fifteenth and sixteenth centuries, and the Incas were Cuzco's mastercraftsmen. Similarly, the only central coastal culture to which I would be willing to apply these names and definitions falls early in the first millennium B.C.

The principal difficulty with developmental stages as an organizing principle is their assumption that similar events happened at about the same time and in the same sequence all over ancient Peru. The archaeological evidence, on the other hand, demonstrates clearly that such regularity was not the case. All but one of the known cities of the south highlands, for example, were built, occupied and abandoned long before Bennett's City Builder stage, and

[5] Bennett and Bird, *Andean Culture History,* pp. 112-13.
[6] Bushnell, *Peru,* pp. 23-26.
[7] Mason, *Ancient Civilizations,* pp. 14-18.
[8] Bushnell, *Peru,* p. 65.

they were replaced by kinds of settlements supposed to be characteristic of the earlier Cultist and Experimenter stages. Essentially, all of the stage sequences listed above define the archaeological sequence of the Virú Valley on the north coast of Peru, but they cannot be applied to Peru as a whole.

As a solution to these and other difficulties presented by developmental stages, John H. Rowe has proposed that Peruvian archaeology be organized by periods rather than stages. He has set up a system of periods for the later, pottery-using cultures. Each of these periods is a discrete unit of time with a definite beginning and ending date, defined by some major event on the south coast. Every ancient culture or event that is contemporary with one of the periods is placed in that period, regardless of its nature. The result is a simple chronological chart for the whole of the Central Andes, without assumptions about the nature or simultaneity of events in different parts of the area.[9]

This book retains one simple stage distinction, that between ceramic and preceramic. These two grand divisions of Peruvian archaeology are stages, not periods, because they are defined by their cultural content (presence or absence of pottery) and because the transition from one to the other did not take place everywhere at the same time. The introduction of pottery making had little immediate impact on the ancient cultures, but it is of enormous importance to the archaeologist. Pottery, when it occurs in an archaeological site, is abundant and easily preserved, and shows rapid changes in style which make it extremely useful for dating archaeological sites and events. Its durability and abundance guarantee that one will be able to identify the stage to which any ancient culture belongs, without ambiguity or subjective judgments. In addition, there is now ample evidence from many parts of Peru to show that, with only one possible minor exception, all of the preceramic sites in any given region were older than all of the ceramic sites.

In succeeding chapters each of these major stages will be subdivided into a number of periods, as suggested by Rowe. The Ceramic Stage periods are those which he has proposed, modified

[9] John H. Rowe, "Stages and Periods in Archaeological Interpretation," *Southwestern Journal of Anthropology*, XVIII, No. 1 (1962), 1-27.

only by treating the beginning of the Initial Period as a stage division (i.e., one which does not begin everywhere at the same time). The Preceramic Stage periods were worked out by Thomas C. Patterson and myself as a means of organizing the preceramic cultures of the whole of South America. The periods are the following:

Stage	Period		Dates	
CERAMIC:	Late Horizon		1476-1534	A.D.
	Late Intermediate		1000-1476	A.D.
	Middle Horizon		600-1000	A.D.
	Early Intermediate	B.C.	200-600	A.D.
	Early Horizon	B.C.	900-200	
	Initial Period	B.C.	1800 ⎫ -900 1500 ⎭	
PRECERAMIC:	Period VI	B.C.	2500- ⎰ 1800 ⎱ 1500	
	Period V	B.C.	4200-2500	
	Period IV	B.C.	6000-4200	
	Period III	B.C.	8000-6000	
	Period II	B.C.	9500-8000	
	Period I	B.C.	? -9500	

The main problem with the use of this system is that of cross-dating or determining how the archaeological sequences of other regions fit with that of the south coast (Ceramic Stage) or with the few well-dated preceramic cultures. Cross-dating is done by reasoning from dated pieces, stylistic influences, and radiocarbon dates. As one gets farther from the south coast, trade pieces from that region become ever more difficult to find and stylistic influences become ever more tenuous, while radiocarbon dates may be lacking or inaccurate. Table 2 is an attempt to fit the major ancient cultures into the period system. It should be read with certain reservations. For the Ceramic Stage, the cultures of the south and central coast are most accurately dated, whereas the period attributions of some north coastal and highlands cultures are based only on a few radiocarbon dates and little direct evidence for cross-dating. For the Preceramic Stage, the soundest dating is that of the central to north coast; elsewhere there is still some room for doubt.

COAST

	Far North	North	North Central	Central	South Central	South	Far South
Late Horizon	Chimú / Piura	Inca / Chimú	Inca / Chimú	Inca / Huancho	Inca / Chincha	Tajaraca	
Late Intermediate Period	Garbanzal / Piura	Chimú	Chimú / Santa	Chancay / Huancho	Chincha	Soniche / Chulpaca	Ilo
Middle Horizon		Tomaval	Pativilca	Pachacamac / Nievería	? / Cerro de Oro	Epigonal / Atarco	Loreto
Early Intermediate Period	Sechura	Moche / Gallinazo / Salinar	? / Patazca	Lima / Baños de Boza / Miramar	Estrella / Carmen	Nazca	San Beni... / Islay
Early Horizon	Pichiche / Paita	Cupisnique	Pallka	Ventanilla / Colinas	Topará / Pozuelo	Paracas / Disco Verde	Ichuña
Initial Period		Guañape	Gualaño / Cahuacucho	Curayacu / Florida	?	Mastodonte / Hacha	
Preceramic VI	Negritos / San Juan	Huaca Prieta	Haldas / Culebras	Chira / Chuquitanta Rio Seco	Asia	Casavilca	?
Preceramic V	Honda	?		Encanto / Pampa / Corbina			
Preceramic IV	Siches	Paiján		Canario / Luz			Toquepala / Puyenca
Preceramic III				Arenal / Chivateros II			Playa Chi... / Toquepala
Preceramic II				Chivateros I			
Preceramic I				Oquendo / Red Zone			

TABLE 2

CHRONOLOGY OF PERUVIAN CULTURES

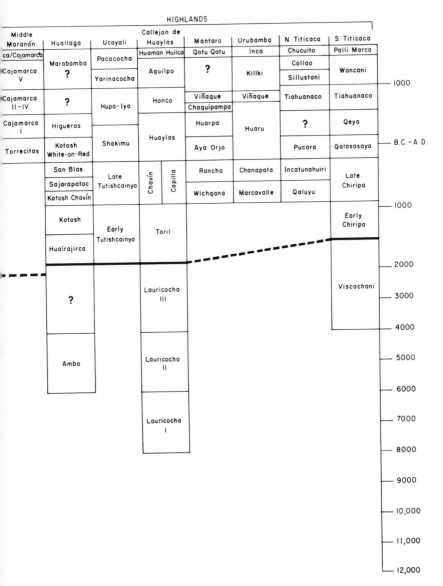

Middle Marañón	Huallaga	Ucayali	Callejon de Huaylas		Mantaro	Urubamba	N. Titicaca	S. Titicaca	
ca/Cajamarca		Pacacocha	Huaman Huilca		Qotu Qotu	Inca	Chucuito	Palli Marca	
Cajamarca V	Marabamba ?	Yarinacocha	Aquilpo		?	Killki	Collao	Wancani	— 1000
							Sillustani		
Cajamarca II - IV	?	Hupa-Iya	Honco		Viñaque	Viñaque	Tiahuanaco	Tiahuanaco	
					Chaquipampa				
Cajamarca I	Higueras	Shakimu	Huaylas		Huarpa	Huaru	?	Qeya	
Torrecitas	Kotosh White-on-Red				Aya Orjo		Pucara	Qalasasaya	— B.C.–A.D.
	San Blas	Late Tutishcainyo	Chavín	Capilla	Rancha	Chanapata	Incatunahuiri	Late Chiripa	
	Sajarapatac								
	Kotosh Chavín				Wichqana	Marcavalle	Qaluyu		
	Kotosh	Early Tutishcainyo	Toril					Early Chiripa	— 1000
	Huairajirca								
	?		Lauricocha III					Viscachani	— 2000
									— 3000
									— 4000
	Ambo		Lauricocha II						— 5000
									— 6000
			Lauricocha I						— 7000
									— 8000

HIGHLANDS

— 9000

— 10,000

— 11,000

— 12,000

ABSOLUTE DATING

The Late Horizon is dated by historical records—the written observations of the early Spanish conquerors and their records of statements made by the Indians. For all of the earlier periods, we must rely exclusively on radiocarbon dating if we wish to adjust our periods to calendar dates.

Radiocarbon dating is a means of estimating age on the basis of the decay of the radioactive isotope carbon 14. This isotope is created in the upper atmosphere by the bombardment of cosmic rays, whence it is distributed throughout the atmosphere and the ocean. In theory, the proportion of carbon 14 (relative to the stable isotope carbon 12) is the same throughout the world's air and water and in every living organism. When a plant or animal dies, it ceases to exchange carbon with the atmosphere (or ocean, as the case may be), and its carbon 14 continues to decay at a fixed rate. By measuring the remaining radioactivity, we arrive at an estimate of the date when the organism died. Radiocarbon dating is applied to archaeology by making these measurements on charcoal, plant remains, sea shells, or other organic remains associated with archaeological assemblages.

There are many factors that prevent radiocarbon dates from being completely accurate. Archaeologists are not always careful in determining the associations of the sample. There are many circumstances under which a carbon sample may be contaminated with new radioactivity or with "dead" carbon. Different cleaning procedures in different laboratories often produce different results. The accuracy of the measurement depends on the length of time during which radiations are counted, and our overworked laboratories cannot afford really long counting periods. Dates are determined as mathematically calculated approximations, often leaving room for divergent interpretations. Dates determined during the early years of radiocarbon dating (1950-60) are often much later than dates obtained from the same materials in more recent years. Recent research has shown that the amount of carbon 14 in the atmosphere may vary cyclically through the course of time. The use of fossil fuels since the industrial revolution has added a great deal of "dead" carbon to the atmosphere. Finally, atom bomb tests may have contaminated samples in some parts of the world.

In order to compensate for all these sources of error, radiocarbon dates must be evaluated by comparing whole series of them. Such a comparison reveals those dates which are far out of line with the rest and allows a balanced judgment of the time range shown by the remainder. The dates listed on p. 25 and in Table 2 are the result of such comparisons. Though radiocarbon is considered to be a method of "absolute" dating, dates so obtained must not be considered absolutely correct. Our Ceramic Stage dates may err by 50 or 100 years or perhaps a little more, and errors of as much as 500 years are not impossible for Preceramic Periods I-III.

NAMES OF CULTURES

The names applied to the ancient cultures in this book differ somewhat from those used by previous writers, because I have made a systematic attempt to select those which conform to the rules of terminology current in the science of archaeology. These rules are the following:

1. Where there is absolute proof that an ancient culture was the product of a specific people, an ethnic or linguistic name may be applied.
2. Where such proof is lacking (as it usually is), the name should be that of an archaeological site, locality, or geographical feature.
3. If more than one such name is in use for a single culture, the first to have been used is the valid one.
4. If one name has been applied to two or more cultures, it must be restricted to one of them or eliminated altogether.

Two examples will suffice to illustrate the procedure. I have accepted the name "Moche" because it is a locality name, whereas the more current "Mochica" and "Proto-Chimú" are both ethnic names, used despite the fact that there is no proof that the Moche people spoke the Mochica language or were the direct ancestors of the later Chimú people. "Proto-Chimú" is also invalid under rule 4, and rule 4 has been employed to pare away other meanings of "Moche." The term "Lima" is valid because it was the first geographical name to be applied (in the form "Proto-Lima"). Better known names for the same culture are "Interlocking," invalid under rules 2-4, and "Playa Grande," a correct geographical term that must nevertheless yield precedence to "Lima" under rule 3. A less-used term, "Maranga," has been eliminated under both rules 3 and 4.

ARCHAEOLOGICAL REGIONS

It has been customary to divide the coast and the highlands each into three sections—north, central, and south—for the purpose of identifying and discussing regional cultures. Only the area of the south highlands has been subdivided in order to permit separate consideration of the zones to the north and south of Lake Titicaca. With the extension of research into previously unexplored areas, a finer regional subdivision has become necessary. Most of the research has been concentrated in fifteen regions, one in the *montaña* and seven each in the highlands and on the coast. The few important sites which lie outside these regions can conveniently be handled by relating them to the fifteen maor zones, rather than by further subdividing the country (see Map 1).

The central *montaña* region is that of Lake Yarinacocha on the middle Ucayali River. In the highlands, from north to south, we have:

1. Middle Marañon (Cajamarca to Huamachuco).
2. Callejón de Huaylas (upper Santa River) and the uppermost Marañon drainage.
3. Upper Huallaga River (Huánuco region).
4. Mantaro River.
5. Urubamba River.
6. Northern Titicaca Basin (the Peruvian *altiplano*).
7. Southern Titicaca Basin (the Bolivian *altiplano*).

The most complete archaeological sequence is that of the Callejón. Only a few small zones have been studied in the Marañon and Huallaga regions. Several partial local sequences in the four south-

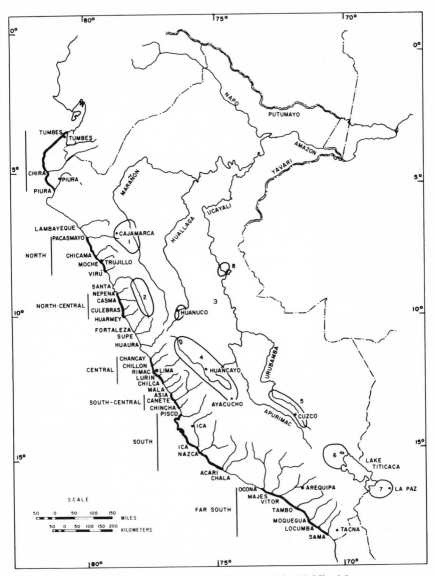

MAP 1. Archaeological Regions of Peru: (1) Middle Marañon;
(2) Callejón de Huaylas; (3) Upper Huallaga; (4) Mantaro;
(5) Upper Urubamba; (6) Northern Titicaca Basin; (7) Southern Titicaca Basin; (8) Middle Ucayali

ern regions can conveniently be combined to treat each region as a whole.

Cultural relationships on the coast have grown so complex that they should be treated on a valley-by-valley basis. To avoid over-complicating the discussion, the better-studied coastal valleys are grouped here into the following regions:

1. Far north: Tumbes, Chira, and Piura Valleys, Piura Bay.
2. North: Pacasmayo, Chicama, Moche, and Virú Valleys.
3. North central: Nepeña, Casma, Culebras, and Huarmey Valleys.
4. Central: Chancay, Chillón, Rimac, Lurín, and Chilca Valleys.
5. South central: Asia, Cañete, Topará, and Chincha Valleys.
6. South: Paracas Peninsula, Pisco, Ica, Nazca, and Acarí Valleys.
7. Far south: Ocoña to Tacna.

Most of these regions are separated by valleys or coastal stretches in which at most one or two sites have been studied. The distinction between the south-central and south coastal regions is based on cultural affiliations rather than on a geographical separation.

SETTLEMENT TYPES

Within the infinite diversity of ancient settlements and structures, certain kinds of living arrangements stand out as important because they are so frequently found in different parts of the country. Some of these settlement types need no definition here. Such terms as "hunting camp," "hilltop fortress," "fish-drying terrace," and "ceme-tery" are self-explanatory. On the other hand, words like "town" and "city" need careful definition if they are to mean anything when applied to archaeological sites. The definition of settlement types involves not only size and density of population, but also consideration of their organization, the activities of their residents, and their relationships to the surrounding countryside. In ancient Peru, six factors are especially important in deciding what kind of settlement we are dealing with.

PERMANENCE

A fundamental difference exists between seasonally occupied camps and permanent settlements occupied throughout the year. The former were typical of hunting and gathering peoples who had to move around after game or seasonally-ripening wild plants, while the latter were typical of the ancient farmers and fishermen.

SIZE

Ancient Peruvian settlements ranged from single households to cities of perhaps 50,000 or more inhabitants. For practical purposes, I have divided all permanent settlements larger than single households into three size categories: below 1000, 1000-5000, and over 5000 persons. These divisions are not entirely arbitrary. Settlements with fewer than 1000 inhabitants were probably all achoritic and unspecialized, and there is no distinction between agglutinated and dispersed communities on this size level. Settlements between 1000 and 5000 may have had any degree of chorism and specialization, while those over 5000 were probably all synchoritic and specialized. Another distinction might perhaps be made at the level of 10,000 persons, since any community of such a size was almost certain to be agglutinated and nucleated.

AGGLUTINATION

This term refers to the density of population in a community and to the nature of community boundaries. In an agglutinated settlement, most or all of the houses were built close together and the boundaries of the settlement are more or less clear, so that we can easily distinguish one community from another on the basis of their physical remains. A nonagglutinated or dispersed community consists of many small clusters of rooms or houses, spaced well apart from each other yet close enough and abundant enough to make it clear that we are not dealing with little independent hamlets. Dispersed communities, even very large ones, have much lower population densities than agglutinated communities. Since they lack well-defined boundaries, it is typically difficult or impossible to define the limits of specific sociopolitical units.

CHORISM

This term is derived from two words coined by John H. Rowe to describe the presence or absence of rural populations associated with agglutinated settlements. By his definitions, a *synchoritic* settlement has a permanently resident rural population in the surrounding countryside, whereas in an *achoritic* settlement all of the farmers live in town, without any permanent rural population.[10] Essentially, these terms define the presence or absence of a hinterland which provides food for a central settlement and receives services from it. This distinction is important for medium-sized and large settlements, but not for small villages. Theoretically, a little village surrounded by individual farm houses would be synchoritic; in fact, there is no evidence that such a pattern ever existed in ancient Peru. Rather, the smaller villages formed part of the rural population attendant on the synchoritic towns and cities.

SPECIALIZATION

The term "specialization" refers to full-time occupations other than raising or gathering food. Specialists might be priests, government officials, craftsmen, merchants, janitors, or people pursuing any other nonsubsistence occupation on a full-time basis. In ancient Peru, nonspecialists were farmers, fishermen, or hunters. A settlement is considered more or less specialized depending on what proportion of its population were specialists. Although any degree of specialization was possible, it is convenient to talk about nonspecialized settlements (those with few or no specialists) and specialized settlements (those with many specialists) as if they were two entirely different kinds of community.

[10] John H. Rowe, "Urban Settlements in Ancient Peru," Ñawpa Pacha, I (1963), 3.

NUCLEATION

A nucleated settlement is organized around a center, which may be a shrine, a plaza, or a complex of public buildings of any sort. An unnucleated settlement is composed only of residential structures, without an identifiable focus. Very large settlements may have multiple nuclei.

TYPES

Using the above criteria, we can identify several types of settlements which, among them, include most of the communities of ancient Peru. Other types existed in other parts of the world, but those listed here are the types of settlement that were important in Peru.

1. SEASONAL CAMP: an impermanent settlement occupied for only part of the year for the purpose of exploiting a particular (usually wild) food resource. Seasonal camps ranged in size from one or two small families to a maximum of about 100 persons. Seasonal camps were typical of Preceramic Periods I-V. After Period VI they became rare and highly specialized.

2. PEASANT HOUSEHOLD: a single small house located on farm land or pasture. There is little archaeological evidence for such isolated single-family dwellings, but they were probably fairly common.

3. MANOR HOUSE: the dwelling of a rural nobleman, usually large and sumptuous and with quarters for servants and farm hands or tenant farmers. Manor houses first appeared in the Late Horizon and are represented in colonial and modern times by the *hacienda* building complex. They are permanent, small, agglutinated settlements distinguished from villages by a high degree of specialization and nucleation.

4. VILLAGE: a small, permanent, agglutinated settlement, with a population of fewer than 1000 persons. Most or all villages were achoritic and largely unspecialized; some were nucleated, others

unnucleated. There is no significant difference between agglutinated and dispersed villages, since both are small enough to have well-defined boundaries. Villages were known in northern Chile during Preceramic Period V. They spread across Peru during Period VI and have continued as a dominant rural settlement type ever since.

5. TOWN: a medium-sized (1000-5000 inhabitants), permanent, agglutinated settlement. Two very different kinds of towns were particularly prominent at various times and places. One, which we may call the *rural town,* was unnucleated and achoritic. The other, the *urban town,* was both nucleated and synchoritic. Whereas the rural town was essentially an oversized village, the urban town was a smaller version of the great ancient cities. They probably had different degrees and types of specialization, the merchants and government officials being concentrated in the urban towns while specialists in the rural towns were primarily craftsmen. Other types of towns undoubtedly existed, including nucleated, achoritic settlements with shrines which functioned as small ceremonial centers for neighboring towns and villages.

6. CITY: a large, permanent, agglutinated settlement, with a population greater than 5000 persons. Though achoritic cities of great size are known elsewhere in the world, especially in Africa, the ancient Peruvian cities were probably all synchoritic. They were certainly all specialized, and most or all of them were nucleated. The largest cities were capitals of ancient states, seats of state religions, and centers of innovation and prestige. Many of them were also marketing centers, but prominent markets could as well be located in smaller towns. Cities usually show clear evidence of social stratification in residential districts of different degrees of luxury and wealth.

7. DISPERSED COMMUNITY: a permanent, nonagglutinated settlement of medium to large size (population greater than 1000 persons). These communities were typically unnucleated and achoritic, and may have had almost any degree and type of specialization. They first appeared during the Early Intermediate Period and thereafter grew in size and importance until, in some coastal valleys, they completely replaced the village and rural town as the dominant mode of rural habitation.

8. ISOLATED PYRAMID, PLATFORM MOUND, OR SHRINE: a single ceremonial structure without an associated resident population but serving one or more nearby communities. Structures of this type are commonly found in connection with dispersed communities, which may incorporate several pyramids or platform mounds. They are not unknown, however, in regions where all of the settlements were agglutinated.

9. CEREMONIAL CENTER: a large, elaborate complex of ceremonial structures, lacking a large, permanent residential population, which served as the focal point for many settlements over a large area. Ceremonial centers represent the ultimate in nucleation and synchorism, since they are all nucleus and almost the whole population is rural. Permanently inhabited only by a small body of priest-administrators and caretaker personnel, they were visited by the populace only on ritual occasions. A ceremonial center may be visualized as the nuclear section of a large city, stripped of its residential districts. Cities and ceremonial centers were seldom found in the same region at the same time; rather, they represent alternate methods of organizing the population of a large area.

It should be stressed that the above settlement types have been defined for the purpose of identifying archaeological sites. They should be equally useful for classifying modern settlements, but they do not necessarily correspond to all of the sociological realities of either ancient or modern Peruvian life. A village, for example, may be an independent settlement related to other villages only through occasional trade, or it may be a tiny part of the synchoritic system of a great city. In this respect, a villager who lived on the north coast of Peru around 2000 B.C. inhabited a social world very different from that of the villager who lived in the same place around A.D. 1500. The former made what he needed and consumed what he made, and probably rarely saw a stranger unless he went to visit an in-law or attend a dance in a neighboring village. The latter worked for the state, purchased manufactured goods from their specialized makers or from merchant middlemen, and took orders from the representatives of empire.

Relationships of this sort, however, can be discovered only after settlements have been classified in a system that permits the identification of archaeological sites. In such a system—like the one used in this book—a village is always a village, regardless of its context. Indeed, it becomes possible to study the larger, complex societies only after we have some sure way of identifying the different settlements of which they are composed.

IV

The First Inhabitants

We have recently begun to learn something about the earliest inhabitants of Peru. Their ancestors came from North America, probably by way of Panama. The country was very likely first settled by groups of hunters or food gatherers moving southward through the long highlands basins. We cannot, however, rule out the possibility of some movement along the coast, especially in the north. There may also have been some penetration from the *montaña*, but this is less likely because Amazonia would have been an unfavorable environment for early hunters and food gatherers. The first immigration took place at least 12,000 years ago, but there is no way of knowing how much farther back in time it may have been.

The earliest archaeological sites yet found in the Central Andes are located in the lower Chillón Valley on the central coast. They are lithic workshops: surfaces littered with debris from the manufacture of chipped stone tools and weapons. The sites are found in the steep hills that rise from the valley bottom near the sea. The choice of location was controlled by the distribution of the hard, fine-grained quartzite used as raw material for artifacts. The remains of such workshops consist of concentrations of waste chips,

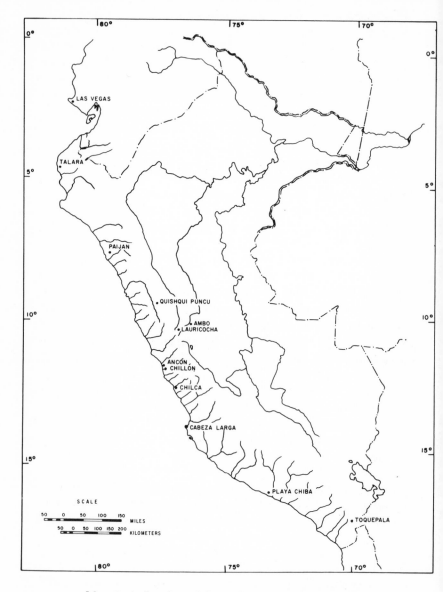

Map 2. Archaeological Sites of Preceramic Periods I-V

cores, and broken or rejected artifacts in every stage of manufacture.

Four successive cultural complexes have been recognized in these workshops. The earliest, known as the Red Zone Complex, is characterized by steep-edged scraping and boring tools made on small, flat pieces of rock. These tools were made with a minimum of effort by striking off little chips from the edges of the flat stones.

The second complex, Oquendo, is not well fixed in the sequence. Its tools are somewhat similar to those of the Red Zone, however, and it probably followed immediately afterward. Oquendo tools are small and highly specialized, and some of them are made on the long, parallel-sided flakes known to archaeologists as *blades*. Along with a variety of scrapers and knives—many of the latter resembling razor blades in size and shape—one finds large numbers of the peculiar little tools known as *burins*. These are flakes or blades with stout chisel-like tips, generally considered to have been tools for working bone or wood (Fig. 1).

The third complex is Chivateros 1. It is known for its thousands of thick, heavy, pointed cutting or chopping tools made by bifacial percussion flaking. Together with these chopping tools and with the debris of their manufacture are found a great many large, sharp-edged flakes, often struck from specially prepared cores and probably intended for use as cutting or scraping tools. There are also a limited number of large spear points, a few scrapers with edges bevelled by fine percussion chipping, and many tools with ragged, denticulate edges (Fig. 2).

Chivateros 2, the next complex, made use of the same kinds of artifacts, but included also a number of thick, narrow projectile points, perhaps used with the spear thrower.

One curious feature of all of these early cultures is the absence of the pressure flaking technique used elsewhere in America to insure straight edges and symmetry of stone artifacts. Chivateros and Oquendo artifacts, even the most finely finished specimens, were all made by percussion flaking with cobblestone hammers.

The Red Zone and Oquendo complexes belong to Preceramic Period I, Chivateros 1 to Period II, and Chivateros 2 to Period III. The absolute dating of these earliest cultures is a question of sufficient importance that it deserves more detailed treatment here. This dating hinges on the interpretation of the stratigraphy at

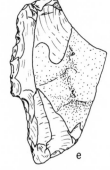

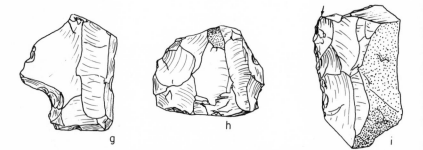

FIGURE 1. Stone Artifacts of the Oquendo Complex; (*a-c*) burins; (*d-f*) small keeled denticulates; (*g*) spokeshave; (*e,h-i*) various flake and core tools

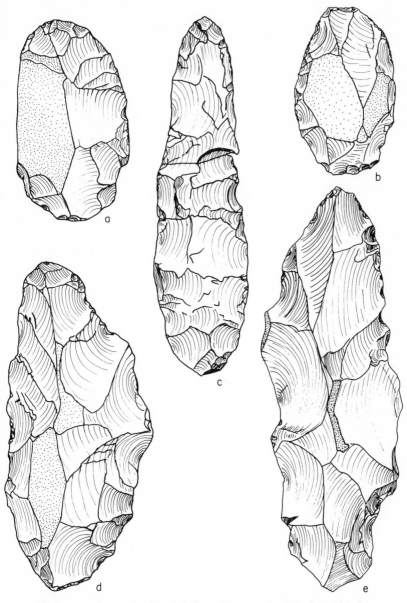

FIGURE 2. Stone Artifacts of the Chivateros 1 Complex: (*a*) bifacial knife blade; (*b*) scraper; (*c*) spearpoint; (*d,e*) bifaces

Cerro Chivateros, where excavations have been made by Thomas C. Patterson and this author. Of the four early complexes, all but Oquendo have been found in stratigraphic sequences at this site.

The Red Zone tools were made during a rainy period, during which a hard reddish soil built up over part of the hill while other parts were washed clean down to the quartzite bedrock. The manufacture of Chivateros 1 artifacts began part way through a succeeding dry period, when fine wind-blown silt was accumulating on the hill slopes. The depositing of Chivateros 1 artifacts continued through a time of increased humidity when the upper part of the silt was cemented with salt. Overlying the salitrified silt are two smaller Chivateros 2 workshops, again associated with the eolian silt of a dry stage. A sample of uncharred wood from the salitrified silt gave radiocarbon dates of 8470 ± 160 and 8490 ± 160 B.C.[1]

With the aid of these dates, the Chivateros stratigraphy can be related to the climatic sequence of the Central Peruvian highlands and to the world-wide sequence of climatic changes that accompanied the fluctuating retreat of the continental glaciers at the end of the Pleistocene Period. Table 3 shows these relationships. It places the Red Zone Complex in the rainy Janca 3 stage, at a time when the glaciers were well advanced. Chivateros 1 began about halfway through a dry period equivalent to the Two Creeks Interval, about 9500 B.C. The radiocarbon dates of late Chivateros 1 fall in the humid Janca 4 period, contemporary with the Valders readvance of the glaciers between 9000 and 8000 B.C. Oquendo, if indeed it dates between the Red Zone and Chivateros 1, must be fixed at the end of Janca 3 times and the beginning of the subsequent dry stage.

We have some knowledge about the Peruvian climate at this time. The summer rains in the highlands were heavier than they are now, and the snow line was lower. Most of the coast was desert, as it is today, but a lowered fog belt and more frequent abnormal rainy years were responsible for "humid" periods like that associated with late Chivateros 1. The valleys were apparently well wooded, and the coastal rivers carried more water than they do today. The northern part of the coast was a grassland containing

[1] Averaged as UCLA-683 in Rainer Berger *et al.*, "UCLA Radiocarbon Dates IV," *Radiocarbon*, VII (1965), 347.

TABLE 3

Climatic Sequences of Central Peru

North American Stage	Glacial Activity	HIGHLANDS			COAST	
		Glacial Stage	Climate Stage	Cultures	Climate	Cultures
1000 — MEDITHERMAL	Fluctuating Minor Advances		QUECHUA Variable	CERAMIC STAGE	Maximum Dry	CERAMIC STAGE
B.C.-A.D.						
1000 —						
2000 —						CHUQUITANTA RIO SECO
3000 — ALTITHERMAL	Maximum Retreat		YUNGA Warm, Dry	LAURICOCHA 3	Dry, Fog Belt Lifting	ENCANTO
4000 —						CORBINA
				LAURICOCHA 2		CANARIO
5000 —	Fluctuating Retreat					LUZ
6000 — ANATHERMAL		SHEGUEL HUAMAN	JALCA Warming and Drying	LAURICOCHA I		ARENAL
7000 —					Upper Silt Dry	CHIVATEROS 2
8000 — VALDERS	Advance	ANTARRAGA	JANCA 4 Cold, Wet		Upper Salitre Humid	CHIVATEROS I
9000 — TWO CREEKS	Retreat	Interstadial 3	Warmer, Drier		Lower Silt Dry	
10,000 —					Lower Salitre Humid	OQUENDO
11,000 — MANKATO	Advance	MAGAPATA	JANCA 3 Cold, Wet		RED ZONE	RED ZONE
12,000 —						

groves of trees, populated by a rich fauna including such game animals as mastodons, wild horses, and camelids. Occasional finds of mastodon remains further south suggest that these animals may also have lived in the valleys of the central and south coast, but for the most part the fauna of the coastal valleys has not been preserved as fossils.

So far no habitation sites of the Red Zone, Oquendo or Chivateros complexes have been found. The abundance of woodworking tools, such as burins, bifaces and denticulates, suggests that the people may have lived in the wooded valleys. The Chivateros people were hunters, using stone-tipped spears to bring down their game, but the bulk of their diet may have come from wild food plants. Certainly the enormous quantities of cutting and chopping tools suggest a way of life in which hunting played only a relatively minor role.

Burins, scrapers, and steep-edged pieces similar to those of the Red Zone and Oquendo have been found on the south coast of Ecuador and in the Atacama Desert of northern Chile. There is enough similarity from region to region to suggest that the Ecuadorean and Chilean cultures were contemporary with their Peruvian counterparts, but there are also notable differences in the tool kits of each region.

Bifaces and spear points nearly identical to those of Chivateros 1 are known in the highlands of Venezuela, Chile, and Argentina. In each case, they come from workshops like those in Peru and, as in the case of Chivateros, the bifaces are tremendously abundant. It looks as if the biface cultures spread rapidly all through the Andes, everywhere replacing the earlier burin-and-scraper cultures. This diffusion may have been due to a wave of migration and the extinction of the earlier peoples, or it could just reflect the rapid popularization of an efficient system of food-getting and its associated tool kit.

HIGHLANDS HUNTERS

Throughout Periods III-V, starting about 7500 B.C., the highlands were occupied by people who lived by hunting the Andean deer and guanaco. Although their camp sites have been found in various parts of the Peruvian and Bolivian highlands, they have been reported in detail only at Lauricocha in the central highlands. Here they occupied caves at an altitude of over 15,000 feet, moving in as soon as the mountain glaciers retreated far enough to make the zone habitable. The refuse deposits in these caves are packed with projectile points, scrapers, knife blades, and animal bones. The points are well made and neatly finished by pressure flaking, and the most popular scraper form is the snub-nosed type, ideal for the preparation of skins for clothing.

The archaeological sequence at Lauricocha is based on changes in the forms of chipped stone artifacts—principally the projectile points—but does not indicate any basic changes in the way of life of the cave dwellers. Certain of the stylistic changes in the artifacts, however, are important for temporal correlation with coastal cultures and with other highlands sites. Thus the narrow triangular points typical of Lauricocha 1 are also common in the Callejón de Huaylas, and rare stemmed points of the same period suggest a possible link to the Arenal Complex of the central coast. Lauricocha 2, dated to Period IV, is typified by beautifullly made willow leaf points and oval, bifacially flaked knife blades. Both of these types are found all through the Peruvian and Bolivian highlands and on the central coast, and in Argentina and Chile as well. Lauricocha 3 points are smaller and often have angular shoulders. They are known from several sites in the central highlands and on the south coast.

The Lauricocha caves were probably occupied only during the summertime. They are located near the extreme upper limit of human occupation in the Andes, in country that would have been overly rigorous for man and beast during the winter. Since hunters follow the herds which they prey on, it is likely that the Lauricocha people were led down to the lower highlands valleys with the onset of winter. In their lower-altitude winter camps they often lived in the open rather than in caves. The open site of Quishqui Puncu in the Callejón de Huaylas was occupied during the times of Lauricocha 1 and 3. There is a Lauricocha 2 open site at Ambo in the upper Huallaga region and an open site related to Lauricocha 3 at Viscachani in western Bolivia.

COASTAL FOOD GATHERERS AND
COTTON FARMERS

Whereas the Lauricocha hunters migrated seasonally from valley to *puna,* their lowlands contemporaries lived on the coast during the winter. Again it is the central coast that has provided the most detailed information so far. In the area around Ancón, between the Chillón and Chancay Valleys, camp sites have been found in areas formerly covered by the fog vegetation of the *lomas.* The food remains and artifacts from these sites all indicate that the primary sources of food were the seed and root plants of the *lomas* and, to a lesser extent, the animals (principally deer) that pastured there. The fog vegetation dried up completely under the clear skies of summer, so that neither man nor grazing animal could have lived there during that season.

In the past, when the *lomas* covered a large part of the coastal plain, they would have provided a good living in wintertime. Grazing animals were hunted with stone-tipped spears, probably hurled with the aid of spearthrowers. Wild seeds were gathered and ground in mortars and rough querns or milling stones. Root plants, such as wild potatoes, were available, as were foxes, field owls, and abundant large snails. At the same time, a small quantity of fish and shellfish were carried up to the camp sites from the shore, sometimes as much as four or five miles distant. The coastal rivers were also exploited for their sedges and rushes, which were used to make cordage.

Once again the archaeological sequence is defined by changes in the style of chipped stone artifacts, but here one can observe a greater degree of cultural change than among the highlands hunters. The earliest complex, Arenal, is characterized by pressure-flaked stemmed projectile points, a variety of well-made scrapers including the snub-nosed form common at Lauricocha, abundant fist-sized core tools, chipped stone awls and small pointed tools, and a very few milling stones (Fig. 3 *i-n*). The Arenal Complex can be dated to the end of Period III, contemporary with the latter part of Lauricocha 1. The Luz Complex of early Period IV was closely related to Arenal, but it had a few mortars and bifacial

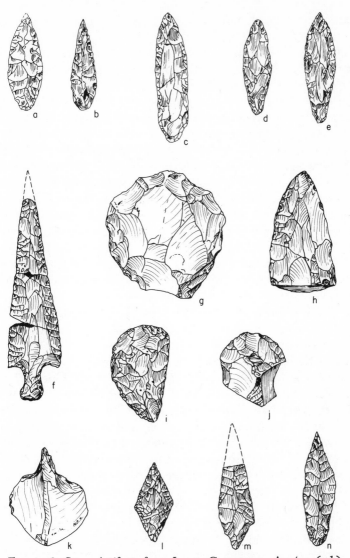

FIGURE 3. Stone Artifacts from *Lomas* Camps near Ancón: (*a,b*) Canario projectile points; (*c*) Corbina projectile point; (*d,e*) Encanto projectile points; (*f*) Luz projectile point; (*g*) Luz scraper; (*h*) fragment of Luz knife blade; (*i,j*) Arenal scrapers; (*k*) Arenal pointed tool; (*l-n*) Arenal projectile points

knife blades of the Lauricocha 2 type, and its projectile points were of the long-stemmed "Paiján" form (Fig. 3 *f-h*).

The willow leaf point, found in the highlands by 6000 B.C., did not reach the central coast until a millennium later, with the beginning of the Canario Complex (Fig. 3 *a,b*). At this time, too, grinding tools, especially mortars, became more numerous, perhaps indicating an increasing reliance on flour made from wild seeds. Canario core tools, scrapers, and pointed tools were few and poorly made, while stone awls and knives were no longer made at all. This disinterest in chipped stone tools continued through the succeeding Corbina and Encanto Complexes until, by Encanto times (3600-2500 B.C.), the pressure-flaking technique was abandoned and the only stone artifacts were milling stones, small percussion-flaked projectile points, and a few simple scrapers made on small chips of stone (Fig. 3 *d,e*). When the sites have been excavated on a large scale, we will probably see that the progressive abandonment of stone tool types was accompanied by an increasing reliance on bone and wood to serve the same functions.

It has been estimated, on the basis of the number of milling stones concentrated together, that the population of Encanto winter camps was approximately fifty to sixty persons.

The only summer camps of the *lomas* people which have been discovered so far belong to the Encanto Complex. One such site is a refuse deposit and cemetery in the lower Chilca Valley on the southern part of the central coast. The Chilca diet consisted primarily of sea food, but gourds, cotton, and possibly some kind of bean were cultivated. Projectile points, milling stones, and limpet beads are all of Encanto types, and the site is best seen as a littoral adaptation of the Encanto culture. A large series of radiocarbon dates place the occupation of the Chilca site at 3600-2500 B.C. Another Encanto summer camp is the Yacht Club site on a rocky hillside overlooking the Bay of Ancón. Here again sea food was the basis of life and both cotton and gourds were cultivated, but guavas and chili peppers were also added to the diet. Twined cotton textiles as well as cotton fish nets were found at both sites. Line fishing at the Yacht Club was done with mussel-shell fishhooks and simple stone sinkers, at Chilca with composite sinker-hooks (stone sinkers with bone barbs attached) resembling specimens found on the coast of Chile far to the south (Fig. 4). A house at Chilca was a simple conical hut consisting of a cane frame braced by whale ribs and covered with a layer of sedge stems. At best it was a temporary shelter, as one would expect in a seasonal camp. Chilca burials were wrapped in mats and laid out in extended position, and were often "held down" by heavy rocks or by stakes driven through the body. Burials at the Yacht Club were wrapped in both mats and cloth and laid in a flexed position with the knees drawn up against the chest.

Some of the differences between Encanto summer and winter camps were a matter of seasonal economy; others are due to the fact that the summer camps have been excavated much more extensively than those in the *lomas*. Gourds have been found in Encanto winter camps, and further excavation will undoubtedly reveal the presence of twined cotton textiles.

Another shore site of Period V which may represent the summer life of *lomas* dwellers is a cemetery at Cabeza Larga on the Paracas Peninsula (south coast). The radiocarbon date here is 3070±120 B.C. The dead were wrapped in animal skins and sedge mats, and were accompanied by twined cloth, nets, looped bags, beads of stone, bone and shell (unlike Encanto beads), wooden spears, and a few implements of wood and bone. Some of the bodies were laid in extended position like those at Chilca; others were flexed as at the Yacht Club. The most interesting aspect of the Cabeza Larga cemetery was a massive secondary burial, a veritable bone pile containing the disarticulated and semi-articulated bodies of some sixty persons together with portions of their original wrappings and some of their grave goods. These bodies had been dug up and reburied, either by the later occupants of the Paracas Peninsula or by grave looters of the historic period.

Throughout the time from their first occupation in Period III until they were abandoned around 2500 B.C., the areas of fog vegetation were constantly retreating as the fog belt lifted. Today the *lomas* areas of the central coast are only about one-tenth as extensive as they were in Luz-Arenal times, and they probably could no longer support a winter population of fifty hunters and gatherers in any one region. The distribution of the ancient winter camps gives a clear picture of the successive abandonment, field

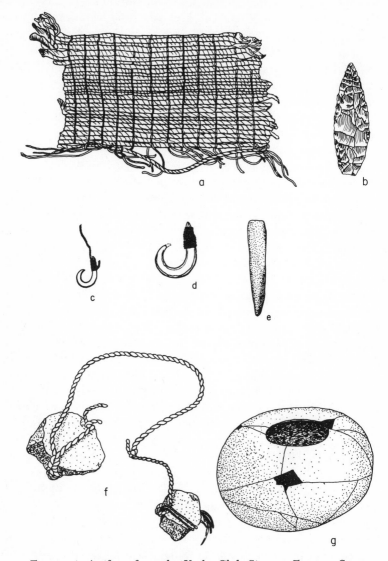

FIGURE 4. Artifacts from the Yacht Club Site, an Encanto Summer Camp: (*a*) twined textile; (*b*) projectile point; (*c,d*) shell fish hooks; (*e*) sandstone file; (*f*) stone sinkers attached to fish line; (*g*) small gourd containers

by field and hill by hill, of the shrinking *lomas*. Fortunately, other food resources were available and were already being exploited by a few people even before the seed grinders and deer hunters gave up their traditional way of winter life, as evidenced by the Yacht Club and Chilca sites and by another central coastal site of extraordinary importance.

FISHERMEN AND SQUASH FARMERS

The Pampa site at Ventanilla on the central coast is a unique refuse deposit which probably dates early in Period V. It lies on a rocky point overlooking what was, until nearly the time of Christ, a shallow bay. The lower and earlier levels of the site contain large quantities of squash rinds and seeds (*Cucurbita moschata,* probably *C. ficifolia,* and the wild cucurbit *C. andreana*), together with mussel and clam shells (the latter from the bottom of the old bay) and the bones of fish, sea lions, and shore birds. The squash remains disappear in the upper levels, which are packed with shells and the bones of sea and shore animals. Evidently the occupants of the Pampa site began as both fishermen and farmers, then gradually gave up their farming and adopted a diet consisting almost exclusively of sea food. No other cultural changes accompanied this shift in basic economy. The artifacts are the same from bottom to top of the deposit: fish lines with mussel-shell hooks and simple stone sinkers like those at the Yacht Club, beads made of bird bone and of thick snail shells, large flakes of basalt and andesite, and cordage of sedge and other wild plant fibers. There is no trace of cotton in the refuse.

The Pampa site is too small to have been more than a temporary camp, reoccupied year after year until six feet of refuse had built up. Though it is only a few miles from Ancón, it is not an Encanto site. The squash remains, snail-shell beads, and lack of projectile points and milling stones distinguish it from both the winter camps and the summer camps of the Encanto Complex. These early squash farmers were a different people carrying on their own life near the shore, and they entered the Ancón region only for the few years when the Pampa site was occupied.

Regardless of the differences between the Yacht Club, Pampa,

Chilca, and Cabeza Larga sites, they may be taken together as evidence that fishing, shellfishing, sea lion and bird hunting, and cotton and cucurbit farming constituted a well-established way of life on the coast during Period V.

ELEPHANT HUNTERS?

The Paiján Complex of the north coast is known from lithic workshops in the desert between the Virú and Pacasmayo Valleys. These workshops have yielded a great many skin scrapers, knife blades, and projectile points of the "Paiján" type that were also characteristic of the Luz Complex. The abundance of hunters' tools and weapons indicates an economy quite different from that of the *lomas* campers, even though we cannot estimate the importance of plant foods until habitation sites of the Paiján Complex are found. Mastodon bones have been found near some of the workshops, but there is no direct evidence of their association with the human remains. If they should prove associated, it would indicate a late survival of elephants on the Peruvian coast, because the Paiján Complex can be dated to early Period IV, around 6000-5000 B.C.

MANGROVE GATHERERS

A highly distinctive group of preceramic complexes on the far northern coast of Peru and the southern coast of Ecuador are tentatively attributed to Period IV-V. They include the Vegas Complex of the Santa Elena Peninsula (Ecuador) and, in the Talara region of Peru, the Siches and Honda Complexes and the Estero site. These complexes are known at many sites in both areas, but as yet they can be defined only by their stone artifacts. All of them have very large numbers of little notched, pointed, and denticulate tools and small rough-edged scrapers. Mortars are the only grinding tools, and they are rare in Ecuador. Projectile points are entirely absent, smooth-edged skin scrapers are excessively rare, and the pressure-flaking technique was unknown. Coastal Vegas sites also yield crude choppers, and the Estero site—which may have been an inland seasonal camp of the Honda Complex—adds polished stone axes and chisels. All of the artifacts except the mortars and rare skin scrapers make up a woodworking kit; the finer tools and weapons so characteristic of other Period V cultures were undoubtedly made of wood and bamboo.

Though both Santa Elena and Talara are now in the desert, there is ample evidence that they enjoyed more rainfall during Periods IV-V, with an attendant growth of grasslands and forest and of mangroves along the shoreline. Siches and coastal Vegas sites are made up almost exclusively of the shells of the bivalve *Anadara tuberculosa,* which lives only in the mangrove swamps. Inland sites, both in northernmost Peru and in Ecuador, are on the banks of creeks that are now totally dry. The woodworking tools—especially the Estero axes—give evidence of a forest cover that is now totally absent. It is clear that the Peru Coastal Current once lay far south of its present position, permitting significant rainfall as far south as Talara.

The Vegas Complex has been studied in some detail, and is probably typical of the whole group of far northern preceramic complexes. There was a clear-cut pattern of seasonal occupation, with rainy-season (summer) camps located inland along creek banks and dry-season camps near the shore. None of the inland camps have yet been excavated. The shore camps, which consist of densely packed *Anadara tuberculosa* shells, are located on the edge of marine terraces near ancient lagoons, estuaries, and mud flats, where mangroves would have grown in profusion. There is not yet any evidence of farming, and the density of shells in Vegas sites suggests that little else was eaten during the dry season. If cultivated plants diffused into the Andes through the highlands (see p. 75), these far northern coastal peoples may not yet have learned the techniques and concepts of farming. Certainly the available evidence suggests nothing but a gathering economy with seasonal migration for the exploitation of particular wild food resources.

HUNTERS OF THE FAR SOUTH

A number of camp sites of Periods III and IV are known on the far south coast. They include both caves and rock shelters high in the uppermost parts of the valleys and camp sites in *lomas* areas near the shore. In all probability the two different kinds of sites represent different seasonal activities—a pattern familiar from the highlands, the central coast, and the mangrove area of the far north. These southern sites are noteworthy for the production of large numbers of projectile points (especially stemmed points related to those of the Arenal Complex and willow leaf points related to Lauricocha 2), skin scrapers, gravers, and drills. In general, the artifact assemblages suggest a hunting economy with little evidence of plant food gathering. The importance of hunting even in the *lomas* camps is related to the fact that the far southern *lomas* were and are far more luxurious than those of the central coast, hence could support larger populations of guanaco and deer. Here, then, we have a pattern of nomadic life related to that of the central coast in its exploitation of the *lomas* and to that of the highlands in its emphasis on hunting.

SUMMARY

The earliest peoples of Peru were varied in culture and economy. After a most ancient period represented only by the biface and blade-and-burin makers of the Chillón Valley, we find migratory hunters occupying the highlands, migratory food gatherers in the *lomas* areas of the central coast, mangrove gatherers in the far north, and possible elephant hunters on the north coast. The elephant hunters, if they existed, were the first to disappear, because the mastodons certainly did not survive into Period V. The Encanto people fished and raised cotton and gourds during the summer, while the Pampa people supplemented their sea food diet by raising squash. Such diversity of food economy must be seen as a response to extreme environments, in which people could live only by the differential exploitation of the few available food resources.

Not all of these economic patterns were viable for an indefinite time. With the gradual drying out of the coast and the northward shift of the Peru Coastal Current, the fog meadows shrank and the mangroves retreated northward until the food gatherers could no longer support themselves with their traditional way of life. It is among the fishermen and squash farmers that we find the seeds of the littoral gathering and agriculture that were soon to characterize life in ancient Peru.

V

Villages and Temples

Starting midway through the third millennium B.C., life in ancient Peru underwent a series of changes involving the introduction of new cultigens, technological innovations, the stabilization of settlements, rapid growth of population, and the construction of great public buildings. Preceramic Period VI has been well studied on the coast, whereas in the highlands we know little about events at this time. Most of this chapter will therefore be devoted to developments on the coast, though an attempt will be made to evaluate what little is known of the highlands cultures of the late third and early second millennium B.C.

The brief period from 2500 B.C. to about 1800 B.C. saw a remarkable development of many of the main features of ancient Peruvian culture. Most of the coastal valleys were cultivated. The total crop list expanded to include all of the major coastal cultigens except manioc and peanuts. Permanent settlements sprang up all along the coast, and some of them grew to considerable size. Public structures appeared in the form of temples, pyramids, and altars. Technology and art flourished in a number of media. The beginnings of formal art presaged the great styles of later periods. Burials were made in concentrated cemeteries, with the body

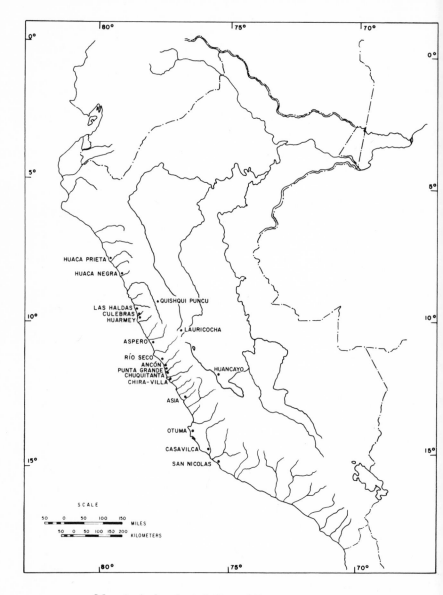

MAP 3. Archaeological Sites of Preceramic Period VI

wrapped in many layers of cloth and accompanied by elaborate grave goods. Skull deformation showed the application of esthetic standards to the human body. Construction in stone, adobe, and packed clay was common. There are even some hints of the existence of stratified societies and of sociopolitical organizations which transcended the level of the village and perhaps even that of the single coastal valley.

Remarkably, these developments took place among people who were not primarily farmers, but rather shore-dwelling fishermen. To the best of my knowledge, this is the only case in which so many of the characteristics of civilization have been found without a basically agricultural economic foundation. Equally noteworthy are the speed with which these patterns spread along most of the Peruvian coast and the burgeoning of population that accompanied them.

Some thirty Period VI villages are known in the area between Chicama and Nazca, and these undoubtedly represent only a small fraction of the villages that existed. None of the known sites can be dated earlier than 2500 B.C., yet all but one of them had been founded by 2000 B.C. or shortly thereafter. Thus, sedentary life became the rule on the Peruvian coast in the brief span of 500 years or less.

Settlements were typically located on or near the shore, either on river deltas, on open sandy beaches, beside old bays and lagoons, in steep hills, or on rocky points. Many of them are at or near river mouths, but others are found well away from any ancient or modern source of fresh water.

Sea food comprised the great bulk of the diet at this time. The typical Period VI midden contains large quantities of mussels, clams, and other shellfish; bones of fish, sharks, rays, sea lions, cormorants, gulls, pelicans, and other shore birds; and remains of tunicates and seaweed. The relative abundance of one or another of these foodstuffs varies greatly from site to site and from level to level within a single site, but, taken together, they are almost always far more abundant than plant food remains.

Another material derived from the sea was whale bone, which was used both in the construction of houses and for the manufacture of tools. In the absence of boats and whale-hunting gear, these bones probably represent the remains of whales that were occasionally washed up on the beaches—an event which is by no means unknown today.

Fishing was done with both lines and nets. Nets were made of cotton and sedge, weighted with stone sinkers and buoyed by floats made from bottle gourds. Fish nets are particularly abundant in sites located on or near open sandy beaches. Fishhooks were made of mussel shell, rarely of clam shell or bone. Line sinkers were most frequently simple pebbles or broken stones tied on with several twists of cotton cord. The paraphernalia of line fishing are found most abundantly at sites located on rocky points or along the edge of steep cliffs. These materials are often completely lacking from beach sites. There is no evidence that any kind of boat was used. All in all, preceramic fishing patterns seem similar to modern shore fishing methods in Peru. Today, some of the finest eating fish are caught by staking out nets off sandy beaches, whereas line fishing is most successfully practiced from the rocky headlands. Modern nets and lines are of nylon, modern hooks of steel. Otherwise, fishing practices have not changed much. Even today's favorite bait, the *muimuy* (*Emerita analoga*) is found in preceramic fishing sites.

Farming—previously limited to cotton, gourds, and squashes, as indicated in Chapter IV—became universal along the coast in Period VI. Food crops are usually found in small quantities but in considerable variety. At the site of Huaca Prieta on the north coast, the residents cultivated squashes (*Cucurbita ficifolia* and *C. moschata*), lima beans, jack beans, chili peppers, achira, lúcuma, and ciruela del fraile. Cotton and gourds were grown for industrial purposes. On the north-central coast, this harvest was augmented by *pacae*, avocados, and possibly tobacco, and, near the end of Period VI, guavas and maize. Maize, lúcuma, and pacae were not cultivated on the central coast until the introduction of pottery. Here, the prominent food crops were guavas and chili peppers, but one site has produced an assemblage of roots and rhizomes that includes at least achira and sweet potatoes and possibly potatoes as well.

Cotton and gourds, universal in Period VI sites, generally dominate the cultivated plant remains recovered from excavations in the refuse deposits. Neither was a source of food. Gourds were cut to form dishes, bottles, net floats, and enigmatic discs. Cotton was used for the manufacture of cloth, netting, and string. The most abundant and characteristic artifacts in Period VI sites—those which give character and definition to the period as a whole—are cotton textiles. Two techniques for making cloth were typical of the period. One, representing 80 to 90 per cent of all of the cloth manufactured, is twining. Twined textiles are characterized by widely spaced paired wefts which are twisted past each other after crossing one or two warps. The second technique is looping, perhaps better known as knotless netting (though the product was cloth, not nets). Neither technique is easily accomplished on a loom with a heddle, and the dominance of the twined and looped cloth at this time suggests that the heddle had not yet been invented. They are accompanied by a very few fragments representing true weft-over-warp weaving, but the latter are both small enough and scarce enough that they need not have been made with the use of a heddle. In fact, many of the "woven" specimens actually combine weaving and twining on the same piece, with the weaving standing out more or less as a means of patching the twined cloth.

There is no evidence of irrigation in the coastal valleys, nor would it have been necessary for the limited acreage under cultivation during Period VI. Farmlands probably took the form of narrow strips along the sides of the rivers and around springs and freshets. Flood farming has been postulated for some of the coastal valleys, but even this technique would have been limited to rather narrow strips along the river banks, because it is difficult to envisage a post-Pleistocene flow sufficient to flood the whole of any of the coastal valleys. Riverside lands could be counted on to give only a summer crop, but lands in the vicinity of one of the rare springs formerly found on the coast might have yielded a winter crop as well.

Agricultural technology was probably related to the swidden system which was nearly universal in ancient America. In this system, trees are cut down or girdled and left to die; underbrush is cleared and burned on the spot; planting is done by poking a hole with a simple dibble or digging stick, dropping in seeds, and covering them up. The soil is not turned over, and weeding is often held to a minimum. Fallow periods tend to be longer than periods of cultivation, so that only a relatively small part of the available land is farmed at any one time.

The latter condition would be unnecessary in the Peruvian coastal valleys where—until the great irrigation systems reduced the flow of water in the lower valleys—the soil along the river sides was renewed annually by silting. Certainly the rarity of heavy duty chopping tools in the refuse deposits argues against yearly clearing of new fields. On the other hand, the only agricultural tools found in the sites are digging sticks. The implication is that planting was done with the simplest of swidden techniques, without turning the soil, but that annual silting made unnecessary any fallow period longer than a winter seasonal one.

Wild plants were also gathered in considerable quantities. The most abundant wild plant remains in the archaeological sites are sedges, rushes, reeds, *Tillandsia*, and mesquite. Sedges were used for matting, basketry, and cordage. Thick, heavy mats and stout rope were sometimes made of bullrushes, which may also have been used for roofing houses. Reeds were used, among other things, as dart shafts and in the construction of wattle-and-daub walls. Mesquite wood and *Tillandsia* stems and leaves were used as fuel, and the wood served as raw material for spears, fire hearths and drills, knife handles, and many other artifacts.

Wild food plants are represented primarily by the roots and tubers of sedges and cattail rushes. Wild potatoes continued to grow in some of the *lomas* zones, as they do today, but it is not known whether they were gathered. Continued gathering in the *lomas* is implied by the appearance of small numbers of land snail shells of the sort which inhabit the fog meadows. In addition, a few of the plants listed in previous paragraphs, such as *lúcuma* and *ciruela del fraile,* may actually have been gathered wild rather than cultivated.

The bones of land mammals are exceedingly rare in these late preceramic sites. In contrast to preceding periods, deer hunting seems to have lost all importance on the coast. Hunting weapons are known, but were probably used mostly in the pursuit of sea lions and birds. The north coast has produced only toy slings. The central coastal sites have yielded a few slings, a few wooden and stone projectile points of crude manufacture, and a few plain and composite spearthrowers. In contrast, the inhabitants of the south coast retained the older tradition of fine stone chipping, and their sites have yielded many small obsidian projectile points in a variety of forms. The obsidian came from the highlands; its presence on the south coast is the only evidence of extensive trade in late preceramic times.

As yet there is no evidence of the llama and alpaca, nor even of the dog, in coastal sites of this period. Guinea pigs, though, are known from the site of Culebras 1 on the north-central coast. Here stone-lined tunnels, running between pairs of rooms, were constructed as cavy hutches. These tunnels, as excavated, were filled with a soft, dusty sediment containing many bones of cavies and of anchovies. Evidently the fishermen kept their guinea pigs in luxurious quarters and fed them the unwanted portion of their catch. Although guinea pigs are usually vegetarians, modern Peruvian fishermen affirm that their guinea pigs eat table and kitchen scraps which include a good deal of raw and cooked fish.

It is difficult to assess the population of these late preceramic villages. Estimates from the size and depth of refuse deposits are doubtful, because the deposits range from high mounds covering relatively little area to shallow but extensive layers. On the basis of an estimate of the number of houses at Huaca Prieta in the Chicama Valley, Dr. Junius B. Bird states that the population could not have exceeded a few hundred persons.[1] My impression, after having excavated in several of the sites, is that most of them represent remains left by some 50-500 persons over variable spans of time. The following list gives my rough impressions of the population of the sites with which I have a firsthand acquaintance. None of these impressions is based on specific calculations, hence they should be treated as subject to considerable error. In particular, the population of Las Haldas may have been substantially larger than shown on page 64.

---

[1] Junius B. Bird, "Preceramic Cultures in Chicama and Virú," in *A Reappraisal of Peruvian Archaeology*, ed. Wendell C. Bennett, Memoir No. 4 (Menasha, Wis.: Society for American Archaeology, 1948), p. 23.

Location	Site	Population
NORTH-CENTRAL COAST	Las Haldas	500-1000
	Culebras 1	500-1000
CENTRAL COAST	Río Seco	500-1000
	Tank	200-500
	Punta Grande	50-100
	Chira/Villa	50-100
SOUTH-CENTRAL COAST	Asia 1	50-100
SOUTH COAST	Otuma 12	50-100
	Casavilca	50-100

Taking the median figures from the above estimates, we get an average population of some 330 persons for these settlements. If we make a conservative guess that there were about 100 such villages along the coast, and assume that the above average is typical, we have a coastal population of some 33,000 persons in late preceramic times. Actually, some of the above estimates are likely to be too low, and the total number of settlements may have been much greater than 100. Perhaps 50,000-100,000 would be a more accurate statement of the coastal population at the end of the third millennium B.C. Though no earlier population estimates are possible, even the minimum figure of 30,000 is several times larger than any possible coastal population before 2500 B.C.

One of the outstanding features of Period VI is the degree of cultural variation from region to region and even from site to site within a region. Each region was characterized by its own architectural techniques and styles, settlement patterns and sociopolitical structure, and by its own variant on the basic mixed food economy of the era. These differences themselves represent the establishment of basic Andean patterns, since the fundamental regional trends of later periods are already discernible in late preceramic times. The most spectacular developments were those of the central and north-central coast, which saw the rise of compact towns and great temples.

In order to give the background for later developments—setting the stage, as it were, for the appearance of the coastal civilizations —the high points of cultural development will be described separately for each region. The descriptions necessarily differ in completeness, partly because of the differing amount and quality of excavations, partly because of differential preservation from region to region or site to site, but largely depending on whether or not cemeteries have been discovered and excavated. In late preceramic times, more than at any other period of Peruvian prehistory, the most elaborate specimens are found in graves and are almost totally absent from refuse deposits. Basically, there were two patterns of burial: (1) in concentrated cemeteries, where bodies were wrapped in many cloths and accompanied by elaborate grave goods; and (2) at random in refuse deposits, the body being little wrapped and usually bereft of grave goods. Most burials in cemeteries were those of adults or adolescents; well over half of those placed at random in middens were children. Evidently the latter disrespectful treatment was reserved for the young and the destitute or despised, while cemeteries were for the use of "full members" of society. The distinction is important to archaeologists. Although any late preceramic site has a few bodies in shallow graves in the refuse, cemeteries are hard to find and have been excavated at only a very few sites. As a result, it is only from these rare sites that we have been able to acquire a full picture of the local culture.

NORTH COAST

Two Period VI sites have been excavated, and at least three others are known. The excavated sites are Huaca Prieta in the Chicama Valley and Huaca Negra de Guañape in the Virú Valley. Both are relatively small, deep refuse mounds, representing at most a few hundred inhabitants each over a span of several hundred years. Both are located by beaches at the mouths of valleys. Fishing was done with nets, fishhooks being almost entirely absent. Houses at Huaca Prieta were one- and two-room underground structures dug into the midden deposit. They were walled with cobblestones set in puddled midden dirt, and roofed with wooden beams and whale bones. Similar underground houses at Huaca Negra in the Virú Valley, where there was no ready supply of cobblestones, were made of large rectangular adobes set on end. Near the end of the preceramic occupation at Huaca Negra, this construction was replaced by above-ground walls of solid clay without adobe bricks.

No evidence of public structures has come to light at either site. A number of burials were found in the midden at Huaca Prieta, but they have not yet been described.

The most outstanding aspect of Huaca Prieta culture is its art work. After painstaking microscopic research, Junius Bird has succeeded in reconstructing designs on many textile fragments.[2] The decoration was done with dyes or other pigments, with yarns of contrasting natural colors, or simply by altering the warp structures. Designs range from warp stripes and simple diamond patterns to complex figures of birds (especially condors), crabs, men, and double-headed snakes. One is struck by the sophistication with which the designs are adapted to the structural requirements of the textile medium. Also from Huaca Prieta come two small gourds excised with designs of human faces. These gourds are of particular importance in suggesting the origin of Huaca Prieta art styles, because they strongly suggest the faces excised on southern Ecuadorean pottery and stone figurines of the late third millennium B.C. (see pp. 76-77).

NORTH-CENTRAL COAST

The Period VI sites of the north-central coast belong to the Culebras Complex, which spread along the shore and lower valleys in the Casma-Culebras-Huarmey zone. The principal sites are Las Haldas, Culebras 1 and Huarmey North 1. Many other sites of the Culebras Complex are known but have not yet been excavated. The settlements were located on sandy beaches or on the edge of the sea cliff between valleys, in steep hills at valley mouths, and near the beach of an old lagoon. Refuse deposits are typically spread over large areas rather than concentrated in high mounds like those on the north coast, though the preceramic refuse at Culebras reaches depths of at least thirteen feet.

Culebras 1 and Las Haldas are the largest, richest known habitation sites of Period VI, and they were probably the most populous as well. This fact, together with the relatively large number of known sites, gives the impression that the Casma-Culebras-

[2] Junius B. Bird, "Pre-ceramic Art from Huaca Prieta, Chicama Valley," Ñawpa Pacha, I (1963), 29-34.

Huarmey region was especially densely populated during Period VI. At the same time, it is precisely in the Culebras Complex that maize was first cultivated on the coast. Huarmey North 1 is famous for the abundance of primitive maize in its refuse, and this vital grain also appears in the uppermost preceramic levels at Culebras 1 and Las Haldas. It is tempting to think that, regardless of how much sea food was being eaten, the population surge was mainly a result of the harvesting of such a productive, storable crop.

Fishing techniques were those typical of the period, differing from those of the north coast in the presence of fishhooks at sites near rocky headlands where line fishing was feasible. The proteins obtained from fishing, shellfishing, and littoral hunting were supplemented by the raising of guinea pigs. These little rodents, too, may help to explain the density of population in the region, since the cavy's high reproductive rate and easy food habits made him an unusually reliable source of meat.

Construction at Culebras Complex sites was mostly with large rectangular blocks of basalt, which are naturally abundant in the region and require no shaping. These blocks, like the rectangular adobes used in Virú and on the central coast, were aligned on end and set in clay mortar. Major walls were double-faced with a stone-and-clay fill. All walls were originally plastered inside and out with fine clay.

The Culebras 1 site shows the most spectacular development of domestic architecture known in late preceramic times. It was a large village or small rural town covering the side and top of a steep hill overlooking the lower Culebras Valley from the south, about 500 yards from the Culebras River and 100 yards from the shore. The entire hillside was leveled off into broad terraces faced with stone blocks, with rectangular niches in some of the facing walls. Each platform bore a few two- or three-room semisubterranean houses, the underground portion varying from waist height to about shoulder height. The underground sections were lined with typical stone-block walls, whereas the upper parts must have been made of adobe bricks, tamped clay, or clay-and-cane construction. Each house had a guinea pig hutch in the form of a stone-lined tunnel connecting two rooms at floor level. The floors were of hard-packed clay. Small birds, wrapped in cloth and set into holes at the base of walls, represent dedicatory offerings made at the time the houses were built.

Burials at Culebras 1 were wrapped in many layers of cloth and mats and accompanied by a rich inventory of ornaments, gourd vessels, and foodstuffs. Most of the dead were buried under the floors of houses, some of which were then refloored and continued in use. A large cemetery on top of the hill has only been sampled by one small trench. All of the bodies were tightly flexed, with the knees drawn up to the chin and the head pointed west. They wore necklaces, pendants, and other ornaments of shell, stone, and bone. Pairs of long bone hairpins may have seen double duty as bodkins in the production of twined and looped cloth. Almost all of the burials were accompanied by bottles, bowls, or plates cut from gourds and containing decayed foodstuffs. More rarely, they were accompanied by such objects as fishhooks or a spearthrower. The skulls of these people had been shortened and heightened by strapping their heads to a board in infancy. This deformation lasted throughout the life of the individual.

It is not yet clear whether the preceramic people of the Casma-Culebras-Huarmey zone had begun to build temples or whether their architectural achievements were all channeled into such domestic enterprises as the terracing of the Culebras hill. It is possible that the building of the great ceremonial center at Las Haldas (see p. 91) was begun during preceramic times, but only extensive excavations will determine whether this was the case.

A nucleated village, known as Aspero, has been excavated near the Port of Supe to the south of the area of Culebras Complex occupation. So few artifacts have been reported from Aspero that its cultural affinities cannot be determined, but it shares with the Culebras Complex a subsistence based partly on maize cultivation. The public building is a small boulder-walled enclosure containing two altarlike platforms, the tops of which had been repeatedly burned. Small subsidiary rooms may have been either living quarters or storage units. The remainder of the site is apparently a large, shallow midden deposit. Aspero, then, was a typical late preceramic village, linked to the Culebras Complex through maize cultivation and to the central coast by the presence of a local shrine.

CENTRAL COAST

The late preceramic population of the central coast may not have been so dense as that of the Culebras zone, nor did the inhabitants cultivate maize or raise guinea pigs. Nevertheless, it was on the central coast that ceremonialism, as expressed in monumental architecture, reached its peak during Period VI. The first pyramids were built at this time, and so was the first of the great temples of ancient Peru. This temple, located in the lower Chillón Valley, was a masterpiece of preceramic Peruvian architecture.

Five Period VI sites are known on the central coast, including Río Seco to the north of the Chancay Valley, the Tank Site at Ancón, Punta Grande at Ventanilla, Chuquitanta in the Chillón Valley, and Chira/Villa in the Rimac Valley. The range of site location—on beaches, beside old bays, in rocky hills, or in lower river valleys—was much the same as in the Culebras Complex, but Chuquitanta was located further inland on its delta than was any known site further north. As on the north-central coast, refuse deposits tend to be spread over large areas rather than mounded up. Cultivated food plants were scarcer and less varied, though they included the sweet potato which has not been found in preceramic sites elsewhere.

In the diversity of their techniques and materials, the people of the central coast may be called the master architects of preceramic Peru. Construction materials, different from site to site, included stone blocks set vertically (as at Culebras) or horizontally, large rectangular adobes, boulders, earth and rubble fills, small lump adobes, and occasionally whale vertebrae and blocks of fossil coral.

Houses were compounds of several rooms, built of stone blocks or large adobes set upright in clay mortar. In contrast to the subterranean and semisubterranean houses found further north, the people of the central coast built their houses on the surface of the ground or even on artificial mounds. The one fully excavated house compound, at Río Seco, would have provided living quarters for an extended family of eight or ten persons. A compound at the Tank Site, only partially revealed by excavation, may have been considerably larger.

Where time and energy were invested in public construction,

they were dedicated to the building of ceremonial structures. At Río Seco, two small pyramids were built. Excavation of one of them reveals that it had begun as an arrangement of five or six interconnected adobe-walled rooms, seemingly a house compound. This structure was then filled in to above the wall tops with large boulders brought about a mile from the dry bed of the Río Seco, together with a few small lump adobes, whale vertebrae, and blocks of fossil coral. A new cluster of rooms was built on top of the mound thus formed, and these rooms were in turn filled in the same fashion. Finally the whole structure—by now in the shape of a rough low pyramid—was covered with sand, and several long blocks of stone were erected vertically on top of it. Small test excavations in the second pyramid suggest that it underwent a similar process of growth. For several hundred yards around the foot of the pyramids, the beach is covered with a layer of shell refuse in which ceremonial caches or offerings were buried. Each cache is a hole containing such diverse goods as bundles of sedges, leaves, roots or rhizomes; cobblestones; clam, mussel, and land snail shells; tunicates, *muimuy,* whole fish, bird beaks, crude cotton, and gourds (some of them cut into bottles or net floats); bundles of sticks, bird bones or sea lion bones (the latter often decorated with incised lines); needles, mesh measures, and other tools of bone; twined cotton cloth, cotton yarn, twined sedge matting, and sedge or rush rope.

By far the largest and most impressive of all preceramic constructions was at Chuquitanta in the lower Chillón Valley. This great complex of buildings covers an area about 900 by 650 yards. It is located on the valley floor, on the landward side of the range of hills where the Chivateros and Oquendo people had chipped their stone tools during Periods I and II. Chuquitanta may once have had a large resident population, but most of their refuse has long ago been destroyed by plowing. The location of the site, together with the scarcity of shells in the remaining refuse, suggests that the primary economic activity was farming in the rich delta land, rather than fishing and shellfishing.

The nine buildings at Chuquitanta were made of natural stone blocks, laid flat, set in clay mortar, and plastered with fine clay. Major walls, like those at Culebras, were double faced and filled.

The three principal buildings were arranged in a pattern that was later to characterize many ceremonial centers of northern Peru: a central temple flanked by two protruding wings, the whole enclosing a large patio that is open at the end opposite the temple. At Chuquitanta the temple is a complex structure built on an artificial mound, consisting of rooms on both sides of a central stairway. The wings are among the largest buildings known in ancient Peru. The larger of them is about 450 yards long. Each of these great structures is composed of many rooms which abut each other in beehive fashion. Unfortunately, neither of the wings has yet been excavated, so we do not know whether they contained living quarters or whether they were composed of workshops, storehouses and other rooms accessory to the functioning of the temple.

Apart from its nucleation, Chuquitanta had a degree of synchorism. It was probably the center for the trading of farm produce to the fishing villages at Ventanilla and Ancón. Two small buried refuse sites in the Chillón Valley probably belonged to Period VI. Their location suggests that they were little farming settlements dependent on Chuquitanta. If the wing structures at Chuquitanta were residential, they could have housed at least 1000 persons, making this the first urban town in Peru. If Chuquitanta did not have a large residential population, it was probably the first ceremonial center of ancient Peru. In either case, with the building of Chuquitanta the central coast now stood on the threshold of civilization, and it had arrived there less than 700 years after its people had given up the old hunting and gathering way of life.

SOUTH-CENTRAL COAST

The only Period VI site yet known on the south-central coast is Asia 1, a small village and cemetery in the lower Asia Valley. A walled house compound excavated here consisted of several small rooms, passageways, and storage chambers, all with packed earth floors and wall bases made of rubble and clay and plastered with fine clay. A second compound, only partly revealed by excavation, had walls of large rectangular adobes like those used in the Río Seco compound. The cemetery consisted of densely concentrated burials in a shallow midden deposit overlying the first compound. All of the bodies had deformed skulls like those of the Culebras people. As at Culebras, they were wrapped in mats and multiple layers of cotton cloth, wore necklaces and pendants of bone, shell, and stone, and were accompanied by diverse grave goods. The bodies were tightly flexed and lay with their heads pointing westward. Burial goods included hairpins, bodkins, spatulas, needles, and other tools of bone; spearthrowers, projectile points, harpoon foreshafts, wooden spears, and a club ornamented with shark's teeth; mortars and milling stones; shell fishhooks; jet mirrors set in baked clay holders; snuff trays and tubes, lime bottles of gourd or wood, lime and coca leaves; and a great variety of plant remains, baskets, bags, and miscellaneous wooden objects.

A single radiocarbon date from Asia is 1314±100 B.C. Although the date may not be accurate, the fired-clay mirror holders suggest a technique picked up from some neighboring Ceramic Stage people. Asia, then, was a very late preceramic site, occupied after pottery making had been introduced elsewhere along the coast.

SOUTH COAST

South of Asia, the known late preceramic sites are all small and relatively shallow. Most or all of them may represent seasonal camps rather than year-round villages. The sites include several small shellmounds, occupied successively, around an ancient lagoon at Otuma to the south of the Paracas Peninsula, and isolated shellmounds near the mouths of the Ica and Nazca rivers (the Casavilca and San Nicolás sites). Only small test excavations have been made at these sites. A few twined cotton textiles and cotton fish nets are known from Otuma and Ica, as are squash, gourds, and *pacae*. But there is little else to link the south coastal sites to their contemporaries further north. They are characterized, rather, by an abundance of small projectile points, neatly pressure-flaked and made of obsidian imported from the south highlands. Altogether, these south coastal sites give the impression of being seasonal—probably summer—camps of people who were primarily dedicated to the old hunting and gathering way of life, but who cultivated small quantities of a few plants. Exploration in areas of extinct *lomas* may well reveal the corresponding winter camps of these people.

THE HIGHLANDS

The known highlands sites of Period VI are hunting camps similar to those described in Chapter IV (see pp. 46-47). The caves at Lauricocha and the open sites of Quishqui Puncu and Viscachani continued in use at this time. In addition, rockshelter camps are known near Huancayo in the central highlands. Because of the wet mountain climate, which destroys plant remains, none of these sites has produced evidence of plant gathering or agriculture. In fact, the only things that distinguish them from earlier hunting sites are minor details of artifact form and the generally small size of projectile points. Deer and guanaco continued as basic elements of the highlands diet, and people continued to live in small nomadic bands whose itinerary was controlled by the habits of the animals they hunted.

There is, however, reason to believe that a very different pattern of life had sprung up in the highlands before 2000 B.C. The rapid development of ceremonial centers at the beginning of the Initial Period was scarcely likely without antecedents of established village life. At the same time, the presence of maize in the Culebras Complex suggests a considerable antiquity for this productive cereal in the highlands, whence it must have been derived. It is likely that there are great gaps in our knowledge of the highlands cultures of Period VI. Hunting camps in caves or rockshelters are fairly easy to find and identify. Preceramic farming villages, on the other hand, could be so lacking in identifiable artifacts in the rainy highlands environment that they might pass unnoticed even during an intensive search for archaeological sites. Again, since early farming villages would have been located in the valley bottoms, many of them may have been buried under alluvium from the annual flooding of the rivers. In short, it is probable that we will eventually find a pattern of village life and maize agriculture in the highlands during Period VI, contemporary with the last of the nomadic hunting peoples.

PATTERNS AND PROBLEMS
OF LATE PRECERAMIC CULTURE

If any period of Peruvian prehistory can be called a time of explosive change, it is Preceramic Period VI. Starting from such meager beginnings as the Pampa and Encanto sites of Period V, agriculture and sedentary life became the rule along most of the coast and perhaps in at least part of the highlands. The population increased rapidly, planned towns grew up, temples and pyramids were built, art and technology advanced quickly, the guinea pig was domesticated, and a great variety of plants came under cultivation. Before 2500 B.C., Peru was populated by thinly scattered bands of hunters and gatherers, with here and there on the coast a little fishing station or an insignificant group of squash farmers. By 1800 B.C., the buds of civilization were opening.

As we have seen, the coastal economy of the late preceramic period consisted of mixed fishing, littoral gathering and farming, with continued minor exploitation of the plant foods and snails of the *lomas* and some gathering in marshes or along river banks. At most sites sea food constituted the major part of the diet, while farming was dedicated to the production of cotton, gourds, and small amounts of a variety of food plants. Permanent villages were established all along the north and central coast at least as far south as Asia, but it is not yet clear whether village life had appeared anywhere on the south coast.

We know some of the factors leading to this fundamental change of living habits. The case is clear on the central coast, where the transition from *lomas* camping to shore villages has been well studied. Here the Encanto people camped on the shore during the summer, fishing, shellfishing, and raising cotton and gourds. The permanent move to the shore was made at the end of Encanto times, exactly when the fog meadows had shrunk to their modern limits and were no longer capable of supporting even small bands of food gatherers. In a sense, the Encanto people moved out of the *lomas* because they were forced out by nature. It seems logical that their new home should be the seashore rather than the wooded valleys. The shore offered far richer resources for the carrying on of the old food-gathering way of life. The Encanto people were already acquainted with its possibilities, because they had camped there and had, in addition, lived near the Pampa fishing station at Ventanilla.

The seashore, unlike the *lomas,* yielded a rich harvest all year round. Cultivation had acquired new importance and, without reservoirs or irrigation ditches, could only have been practiced in summer when the rivers ran full. In order to get a yearly crop, people had to settle down in a single place at least throughout the growing season. These facts, together with the retreat of the *lomas,* are adequate explanation for the establishment of permanent villages and the abandonment of seasonal migration.

Many of the cultivated plants seem to have come into Peru from outside of the Andes. Maize, one species of squash (*Cucurbita moschata*), bottle gourds, jack beans, avocados, and chili peppers were all being grown in southern Mexico long before their appearance on the Peruvian coast, and it can reasonably be assumed that they reached Peru by spreading down through Central America and the highlands valleys of the northern Andes. The earliest arrivals were squash and gourds, which were grown in Period V; the remainder appeared during Period VI. The fact that maize and avocados first appeared well down on the north-central coast, rather than in the far north, is no argument against their northern origins. Excavations in Mexico have shown that the primitive forms of both of these plants were adapted to high altitudes. Their movement into Peru was probably southward through the Marañon or Huallaga basins, so that their appearance in the Culebras Complex simply reflects the first coastal manifestation of events that had already taken place in the highlands.

Most of the remaining coastal preceramic plants were almost certainly of Andean origin. They include one species of squash (*Cucurbita ficifolia*), lima beans, *achira, lúcuma, ciruela del fraile, pacae,* guavas, sweet potatoes and cotton. Of these native cultigens, all but cotton appeared after squash and gourds were already being grown. It is therefore likely that they represented indigenous wild forms which were brought under cultivation after the essential techniques had already been learned. This process, in which the spread of ideas leads to innovation by analogy, is known to anthropologists as *stimulus diffusion.*

The appearance of cultivated cotton presents special problems. Cotton was cultivated in southern Mexico by 3400 B.C., in central Peru by 3600 B.C. It may have been grown somewhat earlier in either region. The Mexican cotton (*Gossypium hirsutum*) is a different species from the Peruvian *Gossypium barbadense*. Both species, characterized by long fibers that separate easily from the seed, were developed through the hybridization of two or more wild varieties. This hybridization must have happened twice, with somewhat different wild ancestors, in order to produce the two separate species. The association of cotton and gourds in Period V, without other cultivated plants, suggests the possibility that both may have been cultivated at an early date in the southern half of Peru, independently of the wave of Mexican influence which so dominated most of early Peruvian farming.

The one domestic animal of preceramic Peru, the guinea pig, does not yet have traceable origins. Possible wild ancestors lived throughout the Andean area and across most of the eastern lowlands of South America as well. All we know is that the guinea pig appeared before 1800 B.C. in sites of the Culebras Complex. We do not know whether it was first domesticated on the north-central coast or whether it, like maize, represented highlands influence on the Culebras Complex. The general lack of *montaña* influences on the Period VI coastal cultures, however, lead one to doubt whether its origins were farther away than the highlands basins of northern or central Peru.

Ecuadorean influences on the Period VI cultures of Peru were more tenuous. The only clear evidence is in two carved gourds from Huaca Prieta, mentioned above. The southern coast of Ecuador was occupied at this time by a people who lived in permanent villages, exploiting the shellfish resources of mangrove swamps and mud flats, collecting plant foods, and practicing some cultivation. In contrast to the preceramic peoples of Peru, they manufactured highly sophisticated pottery and large numbers of little figurines of stone and clay. This early pottery-making culture of southern Ecuador is known to archaeologists as the *Valdivia* culture. Interestingly, the designs on the Huaca Prieta gourds are closely similar to the faces carved on stone figurines and pottery bowls of the Valdivia 3 phase, about 2300 B.C. In fact, they are so similar to a Valdivia 3 piece in the Columbia University collection that they could have been copied directly from it by an observant artist. We cannot know whether the Huaca Prieta gourd carver actually saw an Ecuadorean bowl or figurine, or whether the designs come from some intermediate region in far northern Peru, but there is undoubtedly a direct relationship between Ecuadorean stone and pottery designs and northern Peruvian gourd carvings at this time.

One of the most noteworthy features of Period VI was the rapid increase of the coastal population. Human populations, like those of other animals, increase quickly when they have plenty of food and few natural enemies. Since cultivated plants were only a minor part of the Period VI diet, the growth and multiplication of the coastal villages must be attributed to the wealth of the Peruvian littoral environment, which provided a reliable harvest all year round with little danger of shortage or famine. On the north-central coast, where maize cultivation assured a storable supply of calories to supplement the sea food diet, the population seems to have been especially dense.

The coastal region from Las Haldas to Asia stands out as a nucleus of innovation and cultural development during Period VI. A great many elements typical of the later Peruvian civilizations appeared at this time. Some of them were also found further north or in the highlands, but they were especially concentrated in the nuclear zone. They include pyramids and temples; diversified construction in stone, adobes, and clay; mummy bundles; multiple burials in which secondary individuals were sacrificed to accompany a person of importance; trophy heads (one excellent example from Asia); ceremonial caches; coca chewing with lime carried in gourd bottles and extracted with bone spatulas; snuff tablets and tubes; the development of art in textiles, bone, wood, gourds, stone, and clay; spindles and spindle whorls; composite combs; bone flutes; eyed needles; jet mirrors; earplugs; mesh measures; slings; and a great diversity of baskets, bags, mats, beads, pendants, and hairpins.

Although there was active local trade of foodstuffs between coastal villages and lower-valley sites, there is no evidence of a luxury trade nor of specialized manufacturing centers of any sort.

The only evidence of interregional commerce was the obsidian trade in the south, which is reflected in the nuclear zone only by rare obsidian projectile points found at Asia and Chira/Villa.

It is not easy to understand the appearance of temples and pyramids on the central coast at this time. Río Seco and Chuquitanta are in a region of relatively sparse population (compared to Culebras) and of minimal consumption of cultivated plant foods. There can be no doubt of the antiquity of the constructions. They are definitely associated with the final preceramic occupation in a region where a good series of radiocarbon dates—including several from Río Seco and the Tank Site—have pinpointed the introduction of pottery at about 1800 B.C. Very probably both ceremonial complexes were built between 2000 and 1800 B.C.

The mere existence of these large ceremonial constructions implies several things about the societies that built them. They had enough food to free some people for thousands of man-hours of construction work. There was a community organization capable of insuring that the job would be completed. The monumental works at Chuquitanta were probably undertaken by several communities working together. Public works on such a scale are usually the product of stratified societies in which an upper class orients and controls the labor force of a fair-sized region. In such situations, the division between classes cuts across lines of community difference and unifies the settlements at the top level of society.

In the case of our central coastal communities, the rich littoral harvest supplied the necessary food surplus, and the temples themselves bear witness to the organization of society. The ceremonial nature of the buildings suggests that, if we are in fact dealing with stratified societies, the position of the upper class was related to ritual functions—though such specific words as "priests" and "theocracy" should not be used without more substantial evidence. It is more difficult, however, to explain why the surplus economy and community organization should have been dedicated to the building of temples rather than to more secular activities like the terracing of the Culebras hill or to ritual activities which did not require the building of such colossal, permanent monuments as the Río Seco pyramids or the great wings flanking the Chuquitanta plaza. This is an important question, because we are dealing here with the roots of one of the most basic organizing principles of the ancient Peruvian civilizations. Its answer will probably require many years of painstaking research on the Period VI cultures of the central coast.

VI

The Beginnings of Pottery

We have defined the Initial Period as beginning in each region at the time of the introduction of pottery. A second innovation—the invention of the heddle loom—occurred at about the same time and spread across ancient Peru early in the Initial Period. Pottery ultimately became a major medium of artistic expression and led to changes in patterns of cooking, storage, and even burial. The heddle loom permitted not only the more rapid production of great quantities of cloth, but also the development of the most complex and intricate technology known to the ancient Peruvians. All of these changes, however, were gradual in their development. Neither innovation had any immediate, revolutionary effect on ancient Peruvian culture. Indeed, most early Initial Period refuse deposits differ from their preceramic predecessors only in the presence of rather simple potsherds and fragments of plain-weave cloth. The cloth made on the new looms was not at first more elaborate than that made by twining and looping. Though most of the earliest pots were cooking vessels, Initial Period sites are as full of fire-cracked stones—indicative of the old pattern of hot-stone roasting —as are preceramic sites of Period VI.

Preceramic economies, settlement patterns and architectural

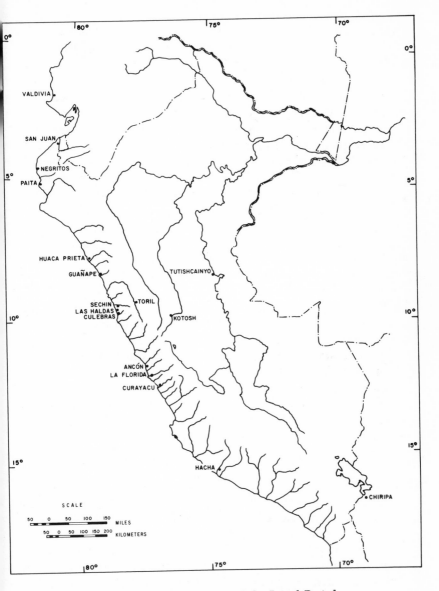

MAP 4. Archaeological Sites of the Initial Period

practices were also carried on throughout the Initial Period. Manioc and peanuts were added to the coastal crop list, maize spread along the central and south coast, and the first direct evidence of maize in the highlands is found. The llama appeared for the first time both on the coast and in the highlands. Temple building spread southward as far as Lima, northward to Las Haldas, and into the central and north-central highlands; and local shrines were built on the north coast. Bigger pyramids were constructed and architectural ornament appeared for the first time. True ceremonial centers sprang up all over central and north-central Peru. Village life took hold on the south coast and throughout the highlands. Cultivated plant foods achieved a more important position in the coastal diet, but sea food was still of fundamental importance. Coastal settlements were still concentrated along the shore and in the lowermost parts of the river valleys. Villages continued to multiply, new sites appearing wherever good fishing grounds offered enticement. Curiously, some of the most productive beaches, such as Río Seco, were abandoned. As in Preceramic Period VI, the agricultural potentialities of the coastal valleys were largely ignored except in the most shoreward portions of their deltas. On the whole, the Initial Period was a time of intensification of the late preceramic way of life and of the spread of basic patterns beyond the limits of their original narrow zones of distribution.

Few Initial Period sites have been excavated. The period is best known on the central coast and at Kotosh in the central highlands. Elsewhere the known sites represent only a small part of the time span of the Initial Period or, where more complete sequences are known, detailed information is not yet available.

THE INTRODUCTION OF POTTERY

The introduction of pottery making in ancient Peru presents many problems, not the least of which is that of deciding when this important branch of technology made its appearance. There are many radiocarbon dates that bear on the problem, but they are difficult to evaluate, partly because of contradictions within some of the series of dates, partly because of the problem of determining whether the pottery being dated was in fact the earliest in its particular region. The latter difficulty is the more easily resolved. In general, a pottery style can be recognized as the earliest in its region when it appears in a detailed, unbroken sequence running from late preceramic times into the Initial Period. Where this continuity is lacking, one can never be sure that a still earlier style will not some day be found. Using this reasoning, we have definite "beginning" pottery only along the north, north-central, and central coast from Chicama to Lima.

On present evidence, the earliest pottery known in Peru is that of the central and north-central coast, from Lima north to Las Haldas. For this area, a completely consistent set of radiocarbon dates indicate a date of about 1800 B.C. for the beginning of pottery making. For the north coast the earliest pottery cannot be dated prior to 1600 B.C., and 1500 B.C. agrees best with the majority of the radiocarbon dates. Indeed, the north coastal series is usually interpreted as showing a date of 1250 B.C. for the first pottery, but a somewhat earlier date is equally consistent with the radiocarbon determinations and more in line with the evidence from the north-central coast. At Kotosh in the central highlands, 1500 B.C. is the most likely date for the Huairajirca pottery of the early Initial Period.

A number of other Initial Period pottery styles in northern and central Peru may be dated by their relationships to the above regions or to southern Ecuador. The archaeological sequence at Yarinacocha in the central *montaña* begins with a pottery style called Early Tutishcainyo which is sufficiently similar to the first pottery at Kotosh that it can be given the same date, about 1500 B.C. In the Callejón de Huaylas of the north-central highlands, Early Toril pottery is stylistically close to the early pottery at Las Haldas and may date as far back as 1800 B.C. On the far north coast, the San Juan style has been radiocarbon dated to about 1850 B.C., whereas the Negritos style can be dated to just before 1500 B.C. on the basis of its simliarity to pottery of the Valdivia 6 phase of southern Ecuador.

The south coastal radiocarbon dates are marked by conflicts and inconsistencies. The earliest pottery here—the Hacha style—is probably not far removed from the beginning of the Initial Period. Of seven dates for late preceramic and Hacha sites, two support a date of about 2000 B.C. for the beginning of Hacha, whereas the other five suggest 1400-1500 B.C. This author prefers to reject the two early dates, while recognizing that earlier pottery may yet be found on the south coast.

The only pottery in the southern highlands which can definitely be assigned to the Initial Period is from the deepest level of the Chiripa site in western Bolivia. The pottery has not been described, nor was it necessarily the earliest in the region; the radiocarbon dates indicate only that it was being made before 1300 B.C.

Evidently the southward diffusion of pottery was delayed for a very long time in southernmost Peru. Radiocarbon dates from the far south coast, northern Chile, and northwestern Argentina indicate that pottery making was not introduced into these areas until early in the Early Intermediate Period. The Initial Period and Early Horizon are represented only by a few rockshelters containing assemblages of small triangular projectile points, which give evidence of the continuation of the old hunting and gathering way of life.

It would be tempting to use the pattern of radiocarbon dates to argue that the earliest Peruvian pottery was that of the central and north-central coast and of the Callejón de Huaylas, and that the later dates to the north, east, and south indicate an orderly diffusion of ceramic technology out from this nuclear area. However, an examination of the early pottery styles and of evidence from Ecuador and Colombia shows that the diffusion of pottery making was very complex and cannot be explained by such a simple hypothesis. Pottery was being made in northern Colombia by 3100 B.C., in southern Ecuador by 2700 B.C. Both dates are substantially earlier than any pottery in Peru, eastern South America, Central America, or Mexico. It seems that we have to look to northwestern South America for the origins of ancient American pottery, and that we must visualize early Peruvian pottery as deriving out of a more northerly area.

At the same time, it is evident that the art of pottery making did not simply spread southward in a single wave of diffusion. The Peruvian radiocarbon dates argue against such a conclusion. Furthermore, several of the earliest Peruvian ceramic styles are so different from each other that they cannot have evolved one from another, as we would expect in a simple process of diffusion from community to community.

The Initial Period ceramic styles belonged to at least three different broad artistic traditions, one of which showed a great deal of internal variety. Each of these traditions was so fundamentally different from the others that it must have been evolved separately for many centuries.

One such tradition was centered around the Gulf of Guayaquil. It included the Valdivia (2700-1500 B.C.) and Machalilla (1500-800 B.C.) pottery styles of southern Ecuador, and the San Juan, Negritos, and Paita styles of far northern Peru. Pottery in this tradition was characterized by necked cooking pots bearing elaborate ornamentation, simply decorated carinated and gambrelled bowls, and the extreme rarity of bottles. The decoration was either plastic (Valdivia, San Juan, Negritos, and Paita) or painted (Machalilla and Paita). The tradition probably reached Peru by spreading around the Gulf of Guayaquil and directly down the coast.

A second major tradition was found along the entire Peruvian coast from Chicama to Acarí and in the northern half of the highlands. Characteristic of this tradition were neckless cooking and storage pots, undecorated or at most bearing a few appliqué fillets or simple incised designs. Bowls were small and had simple profiles, bottles of various sorts were common; both bowls and bottles were usually burnished and both bore elegant decoration in a variety of techniques. Although each region had its own distinctive cooking pots and bowl and bottle shapes, the differences between them were not great. On the other hand, the decoration applied to fine wares was utterly different from region to region. Thus, if we look at the earliest pottery in each region, we find almost nothing but cooking pots on the north coast; dark burnished bowls decorated by incision, punctation and red paint on the north-central coast and in the Callejón de Huaylas; a different style of incised dark bowls and bottles in the upper Huallaga; black striping on orange bottles on the central coast; and, on the south coast, bottles with little double spouts and designs done by resist negative painting (in which the background was blackened after the vessel had been fired and the design area was left unpainted) (Fig. 5). The dark burnished ware and incised and punctate

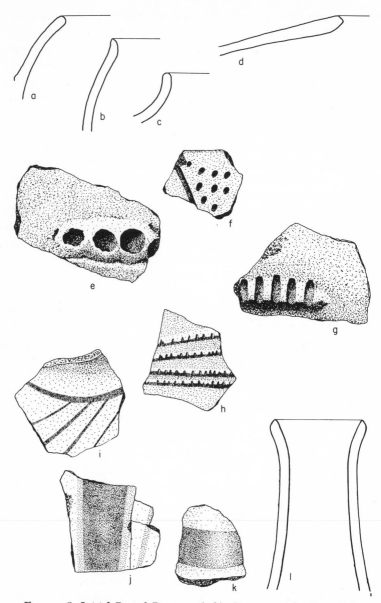

FIGURE 5. Initial Period Pottery: (a-h) Guañape style, Virú Valley; (i-l) Chira style, Ancón

designs of the Haldas style soon spread to the central and north coast, where they were combined with local innovations to create new ceramic styles (Curayacu and Middle Guañape). Similarly, the Late Toril style of the Callejón de Huaylas shows influence from the Kotosh style of the upper Huallaga. Neither of these diffusions, however, erased the strong tendency toward regional differences of ceramic style.

This diversified tradition of pottery making did not originate locally in Peru, because all of the ceramics show a high degree of technological skill; nowhere in Peru is there any trace of "incipient," recently invented pottery. The tradition almost certainly came from the north, but not from the Ecuadorean coast where it was never established. A sea route is unlikely, because we have no evidence of ocean-going craft at this early time and because, when coastwise rafts were later developed, the trade routes lay between Central America and Ecuador but did not extend southward into Peru. The most likely routes of diffusion were up the Marañon and Huallaga Rivers. Unfortunately, very little archaeology has been done in these two river basins, and the only Initial Period pottery yet reported from them is that from Kotosh in the uppermost part of the Huallaga drainage.[1] If the route was through the highlands, it may help to explain the diversity of decorative styles. Haldas incision, Chira slip painting, and Hacha resist negative painting, though quite unrelated to each other, may represent the end products of the evolution of local styles in different parts of the highlands.

A third Initial Period pottery tradition is represented by the Early Tutishcainyo style of Lake Yarinacocha in the central *montaña*. In this style, there was no marked difference between cooking ware and fine ware, and decoration was most often placed on the basal and labial flanges of large complex-profile bowls or cook pots. Early Tutishcainyo shared certain decorative devices with the Initial Period pottery of Kotosh, indicating some inter-

[1] In 1961, personnel of the Museo Nacional de Antropología y Arqueología in Lima discovered a number of sites near Bagua in the lower Marañon Valley which may belong to the Initial Period, but none of them has yet been dated either by style or radiocarbon. One of the sites produced burnished blackware and large numbers of beautiful stone bowls; others had fiber-tempered pottery, a characteristic of the earliest Colombian pottery.

change of stylistic ideas. The Kotosh pottery, however, is too different to have been either ancestral to or descended from Early Tutishcainyo. The latter, found only in the low *montaña*, must be considered a purely tropical forest ceramic style, and this author is convinced that its ancestry will eventually appear either in the low *montaña* or in the Amazonian *selva*.

AGRICULTURE AND ANIMAL HUSBANDRY

The food economy of the Initial Period is marked by three special events: the spread of maize cultivation throughout most of ancient Peru, the appearance of manioc and peanuts on the coast, and the domestication of the llama.

Maize was first grown on the coast in the Culebras region during Preceramic Period VI (see p. 67). It was presumably known still earlier in at least the northern part of the highlands, but we do not yet have direct evidence of its antiquity there. It spread southward to the central coast at the beginning of the Initial Period and reached the south coast shortly before the period ended, whereas it may not have been cultivated on the north coast until the Early Horizon.

The growth of sedentary village life and the construction of ceremonial centers in the highlands (see p. 92) can only have taken place on the basis of a productive agricultural economy, because the planning and construction work must have required a great deal of time on the part of a considerable number of people who were free from the exigencies of food getting for at least part of the time. The Kotosh potters occasionally portrayed maize cobs on their wares, and maize cultivation was almost surely at the base of the cultural development in this area.

Whether maize reached the south highlands during the Initial Period is an open question. The only definite Initial Period site south of Kotosh—the lower levels of the Chiripa site in Bolivia— was a sedentary and presumably agricultural village. Its staple food could have been potatoes, though, rather than maize. Potatoes were the basic crop of the *altiplano* in later times. Unfortunately, nothing is less likely to leave findable traces than a potato in a wet climate.

Manioc and peanuts, apparently absent during the preceramic stage, were widely cultivated on the coast during the Initial Period. They are important, not so much for their contribution to the coastal diet as for the light that they throw on relationships between the coast and the tropical forest. Both manioc and peanuts were native to the tropical lowlands of eastern South America, where undoubtedly they were first cultivated. Neither has ever been grown in the Andean highlands. Their rapid spread on the coast during the Initial Period is the first evidence of contact between the coast and the tropical forest. This contact might have come about by the movement of *montaña* Indians, but the general lack of interregional communication during the Initial Period makes such an origin doubtful. In view of the general isolation typical of the period, it is easier to visualize a village-by-village diffusion southward from the tropical forest of the Colombian and northern Ecuadorean coast. Although the Colombian coastal rain forest was probably not the area of original cultivation, there is every reason to believe that both manioc and peanuts were being cultivated there by Initial Period times. Their southward diffusion would have been by way of the Guayas Basin and thence from one Peruvian coastal river to the next.

Llama bones are commonly found in Initial Period refuse deposits of the central coast. They are abundant even in the deepest levels of the ceremonial center at Kotosh in the central highlands, and ceremonial llama burials were found at an Initial Period shrine in the Virú Valley. The llama was probably first domesticated somewhere in southern Peru, northern Chile, northwestern Argentina, or western Bolivia. Thanks to the vagaries of excavator's luck, the earliest dated finds are all on the fringes of the natural habitat of the guanaco, which is usually considered to be the wild ancestor of the llama. We can confidently expect to find earlier llama remains further south.

There was a definite increase in the consumption of food crops on the coast during the Initial Period. The quantity of maize, peanuts, manioc, sweet potatoes, and *lúcuma* found in Initial Period middens is much greater than that of cultivated plant foods in the typical Period VI refuse deposit. Most of the known sites were fishing villages, but there must have been a very active trade of foodstuffs between the shore sites and the few farming villages in the valleys.

VILLAGES AND CEREMONIAL CENTERS

One of the outstanding features of the Initial Period was the spread of village life throughout Peru. The old patterns of nomadism associated with hunting and gathering disappeared completely except on the far southern coast. Almost all of the archaeological sites that can definitely be dated to the Initial Period were sedentary settlements, either villages or ceremonial centers. The Lauricocha caves continued in use as hunting camps, as did a few rockshelters at Ichuña and Arcata in the far south. In the case of Lauricocha, the "hunters" were probably simply highlands farmers off in search of a bit of meat, but the people of the far south may have carried on the old hunting and gathering way of life long after it had been abandoned elsewhere. At any rate, the dominance of villages reflects the degree to which highlands agriculture and the mixed fishing-farming economy of the coast had become established as basic ways of life.

Together with the expansion of village life, there was a great increase in public construction in central and north-central Peru. Temple building spread northward to Las Haldas and the Casma Valley and into the highlands, local shrines were found as far north as Virú, and one of the mightiest of the ancient Peruvian pyramids was built on the central coast. Nucleated villages and towns continued to flourish, but the most spectacular temples were true ceremonial centers, fully synchoritic and totally specialized. Perhaps the most prominent achievement of the Initial Period was the ceremonial center of La Florida in the city of Lima. It has never been mapped or measured, but the central structure was probably the largest single pyramid ever built on the central coast. That it grew quickly out of the simple beginnings of the little Río Seco pyramids is evident, because its construction has been radiocarbon dated at 1800-1600 B.C., at the very beginning of the Initial Period. The pyramid is built up of many contiguous walls of angular field stones, each faced with clay plaster. Excavations by the Museo Nacional de Antropología y Arqueología, carried out in 1962, revealed an impressive array of subsidiary platforms and buildings around the foot of the pyramid, but failed to produce any evidence of habitation refuse. La Florida, then, represents a new pattern in Peruvian prehistory: the great ceremonial complex which served as focal point for a number of rural settlements but which was not itself a place of residence.

The old centers at Chuquitanta and Río Seco were abandoned before the beginning of the Initial Period, but were replaced by a new monumental construction at the Tank Site (Ancón), about half way between the older temples. This enterprise consisted of a series of large stone-faced and stone-topped platforms covering a fair part of a shoreside hill. As yet only a small piece of it has been excavated, but it is already apparent that the work was on a massive scale and that it was of a ceremonial nature. These platforms, like the Florida pyramid, were built about 1800 B.C., at the very beginning of the Initial Period. Unlike La Florida, they formed the nuclear area of a large rural town.

Three sites on the north-central coast show a different pattern, in which temple rooms were built on low mounds or terraced hillsides, with large rectangular plazas aligned on the flat ground in front of the temple buildings. Construction here, like that at earlier sites of the Culebras Complex, was done with upright blocks of basalt set in clay mortar, the major walls being double faced and filled with rubble. The most important of these temples was built very early in the Initial Period on the site of the preceramic village of Las Haldas, between the Casma and Culebras Valleys. Here there were three plazas, one with a deep amphitheaterlike oval depression. The ceremonial complex measures about 700 by 200 yards, not including a broad entrance highway, over a mile long, made by mounding up the desert sands into a low flat-topped platform. The Initial Period refuse at Las Haldas covers only a very small area compared with the preceramic refuse, and can scarcely represent the garbage of more than a small population of temple attendants. The economic base of the ceremonial center must have been in one or both of the flanking valleys and among the fishing communities of the desert shore.

At Culebras 1, on the other hand, the preceramic village continued to be occupied through the first part of the Initial Period, but the character of the settlement was drastically changed by the construction of a temple—actually a smaller two-plaza copy of the Las Haldas temple—on top of the Culebras hill. This structure may have had only local significance, but it was a most impressive ceremonial complex. The nucleation of the settlement, at any rate, gave it a somewhat more urban character than that of the earlier preceramic village. A third Haldas-like temple, again somewhat smaller than the original, was built late in the Initial Period at Huaricanga in the upper Fortaleza Valley, but here we do not know whether or not there was a large resident population.

Two temples were built in the highlands early in the Initial Period. The Kotosh site was located at an altitude of about 6000 feet on the eastern slope of the Andes, on the boundary between highlands and *montaña*. Here, excavations by the University of Tokyo have shown that a major temple was rebuilt five times during the Initial Period. The two deepest structures did not yield any diagnostic artifacts, but the radiocarbon dates (about 1450 B.C. for the beginning of the third structure) suggest that they may have dated to the Initial Period rather than to Preceramic Period VI. Each temple structure was eventually filled in with large boulders to form a platform for the construction of the next. The most important and best preserved temple was the earliest, which is known as the Temple of the Crossed Hands. It was built on a stone-faced platform some twenty-five feet high. The small section of wall uncovered by the Tokyo expedition contained a row of niches, beneath one of which the clay plaster bore a large bas-relief figure of crossed hands. This figure is the earliest example of architectural decoration known in ancient Peru. If not preceramic, it must date to the very beginning of the Initial Period.

No habitation refuse of the Initial Period has yet been discovered at Kotosh. The successive temples there may thus have been synchoritic, specialized ceremonial centers like those at La Florida and Las Haldas. A similar pattern is evident in the Callejón de Huaylas. No details are yet available, but a temple at the Toril site was built on a high platform like that at Kotosh and may have been a similar ceremonial center.

Another important coastal temple that may belong to the Initial Period was Cerro Sechín in the lower Casma Valley. The site consists of a small compound on a low platform with an outer wall against which were set a row of incised stone stelae. These famous stone carvings show, along with a few geometric figures and possible bundles of weapons, three constantly repeated human figures: trophy heads; bareheaded kilted figures with faces resembling those of the trophy heads; and more imposing figures (warriors?) with tall hats, painted faces, and loincloths who carry scepters or war clubs. The site has never been adequately dated, but Donald Collier has argued for an Initial Period date.[2] On the grounds of the stone-carving style, it cannot date later than the very beginning of the Early Horizon, and the principal choice seems to be between the Initial Period and Preceramic Period VI. It would be extremely valuable to know exact dates for Cerro Sechín because, as we shall see, elements of the carving style make Sechín the most likely ancestor of the Chavín cult which spread over most of ancient Peru at the beginning of the Early Horizon.

The sites described above—La Florida, Tank, Las Haldas, Culebras 1, Huaricanga, Sechín, Toril, and Kotosh—account for all of the major Initial Period temples and pyramids known at the present time. In addition, a number of smaller shrines, undoubtedly of purely local significance, have been found, as well as a number of other buildings. A few of these constructions merit separate mention. Packed clay architecture has been reported from the Hacha site on the south coast, but as yet we do not know whether it was of a domestic or public nature. A large circular stone-walled enclosure at Curayacu on the central coast, where llama bones were common in the refuse, may have been a corral. A one-room wattle-and-daub hut excavated at the Tank Site represents the earliest reported case of a house type which has continued to the present day as one of the most popular forms of coastal peasant dwellings. Finally, a small stone-walled enclosure with an interior dais or altar, at the Guañape site in the Virú Valley, is the only definite ceremonial structure of the Initial Period known outside of the nuclear area of central and north-central Peru. As a local shrine, it represented a marginal reflection of the great developments in the core area.

[2] Donald Collier, "Archaeological Investigations in the Casma Valley, Peru," *Akten des 34. Internationalen Amerikanistenkongresses* (Wien, 1960), p. 414.

Of the seven criteria of civilization listed on page 3, at least four and probably five were fulfilled in central and north-central Peru during the Initial Period. Populations were still small compared with later periods, and intensive agriculture was not yet the basis of coastal life. There was clearly a functioning system for the interchange of foodstuffs between shore and valley, and the ceremonial centers probably occupied the key position in the system. It is noteworthy that most of the shore settlements (with the exception of Tank, Culebras 1 and Las Haldas) were unnucleated villages, whereas the few valley settlements that could have provided food crops to the shore were all intensely nucleated.

The fourth criterion, diversity of settlement types including ceremonial centers, is all too apparent in the archaeological record. The sixth and seventh, social stratification and occupational specialization, can safely be inferred from the magnificence and proliferation of the ceremonial centers. Occupational specialization, though, involved architects, priests, and temple attendants; there is no good evidence of craft specialization in the Initial Period unless it be the carving of the Sechín stelae.

There remains to be considered the possibility that state governments existed in the Initial Period. It is this writer's impression that they did, but that they were very small, encompassing the lower portions of one or two coastal valleys together with the intervening shore settlements. Such great enterprises as the pyramid at La Florida or the Haldas temple could not have been undertaken without the cooperative efforts of many communities. It is difficult to visualize such an intercommunity enterprise being carried out and subsequently supported unless there was a ruling group whose authority cut across local allegiances and permitted the effective organization of labor over a considerable territory—in other words, unless there were small states with their capitals at La Florida and Las Haldas. The case of Las Haldas is particularly clear, because its miniscule population could not possibly have built and maintained the temple alone, nor was there any nearby farmland to provide the food crops so common in the refuse.

Were the Initial Period people of central and north-central Peru, then, civilized? They had the distributive systems, settlement types, political systems, social stratification, and occupational specialization characteristic of civilizations, but (at least on the coast) they were not yet so numerous nor so dependent on agriculture as other civilized peoples. Whether or not one calls them civilized depends on the importance that one attaches to one or another of the listed criteria. I am especially impressed—and undoubtedly biased—by their tremendous achievements in the field of monumental public architecture, and by the social, political, and economic implications of those achievements. On this basis, I would venture that civilization first came to Peru about 1800 B.C., and that it first appeared in both the coastal and highlands zones of central and north-central Peru.

REGIONAL CULTURES

The spread of village life, maize agriculture, pottery, and the heddle loom gave a more or less uniform character to the Initial Period cultures. Within this broad culture area, there was a strong divisive trend in the intensification of the regional isolation and differentiation so evident in Preceramic Period VI. Clearly defined regional cultures emerged during the Initial Period, each with its own style in pottery and architecture, its own tool typology and settlement patterns. For the most part these regional differences were those already evident at the end of the Preceramic Stage, with the lines of division more clearly drawn because of the strikingly different regional styles in pottery and architecture. Except for the obsidian trade in the south, there is absolutely no evidence of commerce between regions. Localized states, if they existed, lay strictly within the boundaries of single cultural regions. In short, life during the Initial Period was circumscribed by cultural and geographical barriers, and people were content not to look far beyond them.

VII

The Chavín Cult

Some time around 900 B.C. the first of the "great styles" of ancient art and architecture spread across almost the whole northern half of Peru. The style is called *Chavín* after the famous temple of Chavín de Huántar. It is found in archaeological sites in all parts of the coastal valleys from Lambayeque in the north to Chilca in the south (i.e., the whole of the north, north-central, and central coast), and in the Callejón de Huaylas, upper Marañon, and upper Huallaga basins. Influences of the Chavín style also spread across the south coast, and one Chavín-influenced pottery bottle has even been found in the southern highlands of Ecuador. In Peru, only the far south coast and the southern highlands basins seem to have remained outside the Chavín sphere of influence.

Stone carvings were the major medium of Chavín art. The typical Chavín carving is an intricate interweaving of mouths, eyes, snakes, and geometric figures in stylized relationships to a central human, animal, or deity figure. John H. Rowe has shown that the labyrinthine complexity of Chavín carvings was due to the use of a code of visual metaphors that he calls *kennings,* in which hair was represented as snakes, tails and legs as tongues, belts and back-

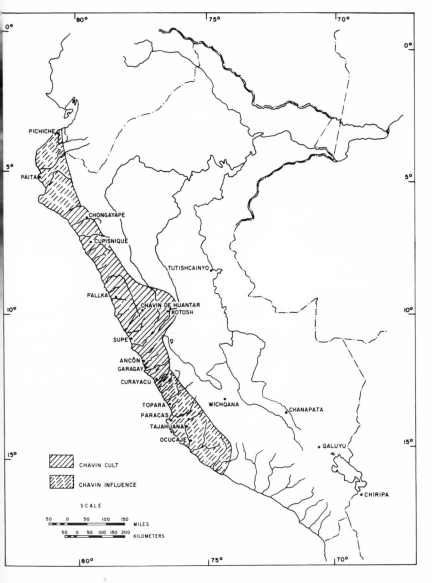

MAP 5. Archaeological Sites of the Early Horizon

bones as mouths, and so forth.[1] The kenning tongues and mouths, in turn, had to be identified by adding other facial features, so that a really complex Chavín carving might have dozens of partial or complete secondary faces at key points on the body of the main figure, together with snakes, eyes, extra-long mouths, double faces, and other kennings. Almost all mouths, even those of birds and men, were shown as fanged jaguar mouths. Eyes were typically eccentric, with the pupil shown at the top of the eye opening rather than in the center.

The most frequent central figures on the stone carvings were such ferocious animals as hawks, eagles, and jaguars. Human figures were also shown, occasionally without kennings. The most elaborate masterpieces, however, were those which showed one of two deities, the *Smiling God* and the *Staff God* [2] (Plate 1).

Lesser art works in pottery, bone, cloth, stone, shell, and repoussé gold occasionally showed the same central animal or human figures, but more frequently they featured secondary figures, individual kennings, or such facial parts as a single eye, eyebrow or mouth.

It has long been recognized that the Chavín style was the artistic manifestation of a religious cult, and that the spread of the style was due to the spread of the cult at the expense of older local religions. Not only were deities and mythological figures prominent in all media, but the greatest masterpieces of Chavín art were the cult objects, friezes, lintels, columns, cornices, and altars of temples. The temples themselves—elaborate structures built on high platform mounds, often with wings outlining a central patio—represent an architectural style which spread along with the decorative style in other media. Chavín temples differ in their construction materials (dressed stone in the highlands, field stones or adobes on the coast) and in the media of their ornamentation (stone carvings in the highlands, plaster friezes and clay figures on the coast), but they show a basic unity of plan and concept which emphasizes the religious nature of the Chavín style.

There is every reason to believe that the Chavín cult originated in north-central Peru and that it spread very rapidly throughout

---

[1] John H. Rowe, *Chavín Art, an Inquiry into its Form and Meaning* (New York: The Museum of Primitive Art, 1962), pp. 14-17.

[2] *Ibid.*, pp. 19-20.

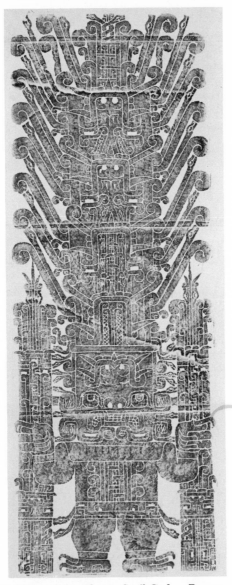

PLATE 1. Rubbing of the Chavín Staff God as Represented on the Raimondi Stele (*Courtesy of the Museum of Primitive Art*)

the northern half of the country. The earliest Chavín objects in each region are all in a single style, that which Rowe calls the AB style.[3] Most of these objects are pottery vessels, characterized not only by the Chavín designs but also by a number of particular vessel shapes and decorative conventions which seem to imitate the massive effects of carved stone. This style was so uniform wherever it occurred that little time could have elapsed during its diffusion. If the process began about 900 B.C., it must have been completed before 800 B.C.

We cannot yet identify the exact place of origin of the Chavín cult. It definitely was not on the central or south coast or in the upper Huallaga basin, because in each of these regions the Chavín style (or elements of it, on the south coast) appeared suddenly, without antecedents, as an intrusive complex that was soon blended with the older local styles. Numerous theories about Chavín origins have been proposed. Julio C. Tello felt that the cult originated in the *montaña* and spread first to the highlands and then to the coast.[4] Rafael Larco Hoyle, on the other hand, proposed a north-central coastal origin in the Nepeña Valley.[5] More recently, a number of Mexican archaeologists have maintained that the Chavín cult was derived from the early Olmec culture of southern Mexico.[6] Still another possible origin, never formally proposed but considered likely by many of today's Peruvianists, was in the north-central highlands.

Neither *montaña* nor Mexican origins are at all likely. No Chavín sites have ever been found in the *montaña* proper, and at the nearest site, Kotosh, the Chavín cult appeared as a definitely intrusive complex. The estimated date of the Chavín diffusion, 900 B.C., is slightly older than the beginning of the Olmec culture, at

[3] *Ibid.*, p. 12.

[4] Julio C. Tello, *Chavín, Cultura Matriz de la Civilización Andina,* Publicación Antropológica del Archivo "Julio C. Tello," II (Lima: Universidad Nacional Mayor de San Marcos, 1960), 36-37.

[5] Rafael Larco Hoyle, *Los Cupisniques* (Lima: Casa Editora "La Crónica" y "Variedades" S.A., 1941), p. 8.

[6] Muriel Porter, *Tlatilco and the Preclassic Cultures of the New World,* Viking Fund Publications in Anthropology, No. 19 (New York: Wenner-Gren Foundation for Anthropological Research, Inc., 1953); Michael D. Coe, "An Olmec Design on an Early Peruvian Vessel," *American Antiquity,* XXVII, No. 4 (1962), 579-80.

least insofar as the latter is now known. In addition, there are clear-cut antecedents for the Chavín cult in the Initial Period of northern Peru, some of them far more ancient than any possible ancestral complexes in Mexico. Chavín platform-mound temples were derived from the Initial Period highlands tradition evidenced at Kotosh and Toril (see p. 92). The stone carvings are related to those at Cerro Sechín by such features as the eccentric eye, face paint, loincloths, and the details of hands and feet. The principal difference is the lack of kennings and of feline mouths at Cerro Sechín. Since Sechín was probably earlier than the spread of the Chavín cult, we need look no farther than the Casma Valley for the origins of Chavín stone carving techniques and representational designs. Finally, the widespread Chavín ceramic style was related to a number of Initial Period styles in the northern half of Peru, though one of its most popular vessel forms, the stirrup spout bottle, was probably originally derived from the Machalilla style of southern Ecuador.

The principal problem is to locate the precise place where these various patterns were fused together into the Chavín style, and this we cannot yet do. The place must have been in the northern half of Peru, because all of the antecedents were northern. It was probably in the north-central part of the country, in the area of the Casma and Nepeña Valleys, the Callejón de Huaylas, and the upper drainage of the Marañon. The Initial Period platform mounds and the Cerro Sechín stone carvings were located in this area, as were a number of local ceramic styles which shared many features with the later Chavín pottery. In addition, almost all of the Chavín figures with kennings have been found in the north-central area. Elsewhere we find either unkenned felines, hawks, and eagles; figures taken from kennings rather than from the central figures in Chavín carvings; or figures with a few kennings which do not make much sense as visual metaphors and which apparently represent local misunderstanding of the use of kennings.

Within the north-central area, it is not yet possible to decide whether the Chavín cult had its beginnings in the highlands or on the coast. The question is an important one, because the later movements that unified all of ancient Peru originated in the highlands. We need to know whether the desert civilizations of the coast ever extended their influence to a large part of the highlands, or whether such expansive energies were exclusive to the civilizations of the great highlands basins.

The rapid spread of the Chavín cult, and its far-reaching effects on the local cultures within its territory, leave one to speculate whether the cult spread only through proselytism or whether it was carried by force of arms. There does not seem to have been a Chavín "empire" comparable to the empires of the Middle and Late Horizons. Neither garrison quarters, secular administrative centers, government warehouses, nor fortresses have ever been reported in association with the Chavín style. Specimens—especially pottery bottles and bowls—in pure Chavín style have been found throughout the northern and central coast and the north-central highlands. However, when we compare their distribution to that of Inca specimens during the Late Horizon (see p. 170), we see that they were not especially concentrated in possible administrative centers nor in the residential sites of an identifiable nobility. Rather, both Chavín and local styles are always found mixed together both in village sites and in the temples and ceremonial centers which represented the public aspect of Chavín life. There was, then, no clear-cut distinction between conquerors and provincial people, and hence no evidence of empire.

Nevertheless, we cannot rule out the possibility that the Chavín cult was spread through conquest as well as conversion. The very rapidity of its diffusion requires more of an explanation than simply successful missionaries. In later times, the Incas did not distinguish between the success of their armies and the success of their gods. Rather, a military victory was understood to reflect the superiority of the victor's gods, and the losers were likely to seek the protection of gods who had shown themselves invincible. If a similar process occurred in the Early Horizon, the conquerors were probably content to build their temples in the lands they had taken and made no attempt to incorporate this territory under a central imperial government.

If the nature of the Chavín diffusion and its exact point of origin are not yet known, its effects are nevertheless clear in the archaeological record. Just as the Initial Period was a time of regional isolation and restricted trade, so the early part of the Early Horizon—the time of the Chavín diffusion—was a period when all of the old barriers fell, when goods and ideas were exchanged through much of ancient Peru. Commerce, such as we know it from the excavated sites, was in art objects such as pottery vessels and carved bones. The widely diffused cultural patterns that we can trace were of an artistic, architectural, and religious nature.

We have yet to consider the question of whether the Chavín temples were the nuclei of urban settlements or whether they were "empty" ceremonial centers like La Florida and Las Haidas. There is less evidence for judging them than there was for the Initial Period temples. At least nine major Chavín temples are known, and others are hinted at in the archaeological literature. Most of them were probably ceremonial centers, used periodically by the rural population but not themselves the sites of population concentrations. Extensive occupation refuse has been reported near the temple of Chavín de Huántar in the upper Marañon drainage, and there is apparently also some refuse at the Pallka temple in the Casma Valley. Chavín de Huántar seems to have been a true urban town or perhaps even a synchoritic city. Some of the temples, such as Garagay in the Chillón Valley, seem to lack associated garbage dumps.

The over-all Chavín pattern was probably much the same as that of central and north-central Peru during the Initial Period, some of the temples being true ceremonial centers and others the nuclei of small semi-urban towns or large villages, both sorts coexisting with unnucleated villages and rural towns. As in the Initial Period, probably only the ceremonial centers were fully synchoritic.

Despite the revolutionary effects of the Chavín cult as a homogenizer of culture, its effect on settlement patterns was only to spread already established patterns into a few new regions. Temples, formerly found only up to the Casma Valley and the Callejón de Huaylas, began to be built as far north as the Lambayeque Valley, but there is no evidence of an equivalent southward movement. On present evidence, it looks as if the middle and upper parts of the coastal valleys were occupied for the first time near the beginning of the Early Horizon—at least, no earlier sites have yet been reported from these narrow canyons. The temples, however, con-

tinued to be located in the highlands valleys and down on the
deltas of the coastal rivers.

OUTLYING AREAS

The Chavín cult proper, with its temples and ceremonial centers, its deities and mythological beings, its stone carvings and
characteristic ceramic style, spread throughout central and northern
Peru. The little-known cultures of the far north coast were related to those of Ecuador throughout the Early Horizon and most
of the Early Intermediate Period, and generally showed no particular similarity to any of the other northern Peruvian cultures of the
time. However, the Paita D culture of Piura and the Pichiche culture of Tumbes incorporated a few Chavín design elements in their
pottery styles.

On the other hand, the cultures of the south coast were
strongly influenced, particularly in their art styles, by that of
Chavín. The Paracas culture, in particular, adopted many of the
Chavín mythological figures, making them the primary motifs on
its pottery and textiles throughout most of the Early Horizon
(Plate 2). No specimens in pure Chavín style are known from
Paracas territory, however, and the two styles are strikingly different in their general characteristics. Chavín pottery was a thick,
somber ware, made in shapes that suggest carved stone. It was
decorated primarily by varying the texture and made almost no
use of painted designs. In contrast, Paracas pottery was brightly
painted with resin-based pigments after the vessels had been fired.
Thus a Chavín feline or hawk took on a very different visual character in the two areas. Similarly, no Chavín temples have ever been
found on the south coast. Indeed, no temples of any kind have
been reported from that area until very late in the Early Horizon.

The great river basins and plateaus of the south highlands seem
to have been entirely free from Chavín influence. The known
Early Horizon sites in the Mantaro and Urubamba basins and in
the Titicaca area all seem to have been farming villages. They
shared a tradition of rather sophisticated painted pottery, and none
of them shows the least trace of Chavín ceremonialism. Similarly,
the late Tutishcainyo culture of the Middle Ucayali in the

montaña represents a continuation of the Initial Period tradition without Chavín influence.

The absence of ceremonial architecture outside of the Chavín area proper is striking. Until near the very end of the Early Horizon, all of the major temples and ceremonial centers lay within the boundaries of Chavín territory. There can be no doubt that

PLATE 2. Early Paracas Bottle Bearing a Resin-painted Chavín Design (*Courtesy of the Museum of Primitive Art*)

the spread of temple building into northern Peru was a function of the movement of the Chavín cult into that area. On the other hand, the spread of settlements into the coastal valleys and the multiplication of villages in the highlands basins cannot be attributed to the diffusion of the Chavín cult. The river valleys of the far north coast, which were outside the Chavín sphere of influence, were occupied at this time, as were those of the south coast, where the full Chavín cult was never expressed. The growth and multiplication of agricultural settlements was as characteristic of the south highlands in the Early Horizon as it was of the Chavín-dominated northern highlands. We must therefore look for another explanation of the spreading pattern of village life. This explanation is to be found in the population expansion which rose out of the productivity and reliability of maize and potato agriculture and littoral harvesting. Coastal settlements multiplied until every good fishing station was occupied by a village, and only then, when the possibilities of the littoral harvesting pattern had reached their limits, did people begin to move into the valleys in large numbers and to take up the life of full-time farmers. In the highlands, the Chavín florescence must be seen as the effect of an agricultural way of life, not as the cause of its dissemination. Agriculture and village life preceded the spread of the Chavín cult, and were necessary to its development and diffusion.

THE AFTERMATH

During the course of the Early Horizon, region after region seems to have broken free from the Chavín influence and to have developed its own art style and its own distinctive cultural unity. Some of the Chavín temples, especially that at Chavín de Huántar, were in use throughout the Early Horizon. Nevertheless, all traces of the Chavín cult disappeared from the central coast and from Kotosh quite early in the period. On the southern and northern coasts, on the other hand, Chavín mythological designs were made on pottery and in other media almost until the end of the Early Horizon.

New regional cultures had sprung up throughout ancient Peru by the end of the Early Horizon. Within the area of Chavín influence, these new cultures were blends of Chavín patterns and of older local traditions. In their art styles and settlement patterns, they were as different from each other as had been the regional cultures of the Initial Period. They shared a common technological and economic base, however, and they were not so isolated as their predecessors. Long-range trade seems to have died out before the end of the Early Horizon, but never again in the history of Peru was there to be a period when interregional commerce was absent.

Thus, archaeological sites of the late Early Horizon typically contain some trade specimens from neighboring valleys or nearby regions.

Some of these changes have been studied in detail at the Tank Site and at Curayacu on the central coast. At Curayacu there was a village refuse heap twenty-eight feet deep which was deposited during the late Initial Period and the early part of the Early Horizon. The deposit, typical of coastal middens of its time, consisted of black ash-stained earth containing fire-cracked stones; shells; bones of fish, birds, sea lions, and llamas; cotton, maize, peanuts, squash, gourds, *lúcuma,* manioc, and other remains of cultivated plants; fragments of pottery, woven cotton textiles, and assorted tools of bone, wood, and stone. The Initial Period pottery of Curayacu was in pure central coast style, specializing in incised and painted decoration, especially on the interior of shallow plates, and in over-all geometric ornamentation rather than in the representation of natural figures. No trade pieces of any kind were found in the Initial Period deposit. At the beginning of the Early Horizon, there was a sudden influx of Chavín designs and of Chavín trade pieces. Other than specimens in pure Chavín style, undoubtedly imported from the north, the Chavín texturing devices and mythological designs began to appear on native pottery vessels and bone carvings. At the same time, non-Chavín trade wares from the south coast and from the highlands appeared in the refuse deposit. The mythological designs were made for only a brief period—no more than a century or two. Thereafter, the Curayacu potters used only the Chavín texturing devices, employing them to ornament the entire exterior surface of their vessels as they had formerly ornamented the interiors with incising and painting. The ceremonial aspects of the Chavín cult disappeared entirely.

At the Tank Site we can trace the rise of the new ceramic style and the new regional culture of the central coast. Here, after a Chavín period as brief as that of Curayacu, the Chavín artistic devices were dropped one by one until a simple but elegant new ceramic style was evolved. This style still shows its Chavín ancestry in its thick, dark burnished ware, its emphasis on a few texturing techniques, and the absence of the old traditional interior decoration and painted designs. As the stylistic evolution progressed, trade pottery from other regions became rare and finally disappeared altogether. The only Chavín temple known on the central coast, that at Garagay in the Chillón Valley, was probably in use only during the early part of the Early Horizon.

On the south coast, where northern trade wares were always rare or absent, a different process is evident. Chavín mythological designs were reproduced on Paracas pottery for a very long time (Plate 2). Changes in the details of the figures faithfully reflected style changes on the stone carvings at Chavín de Huántar, thus indicating that the Paracas potters were in contact with the central Chavín area and were aware of events there. Late in the Early Horizon, the Chavín figures began to be replaced by more realistic bird, animal, and human figures of local invention. Finally, just before the end of the period, the Chavín designs disappeared altogether, and the Paracas artists began to paint new mythological beings of purely local origin. Thus, the Chavín tradition of representing animals, birds, people, and gods was carried on, but the particular figures shown on late Paracas art owe nothing to the inspiration of the Chavín cult.

The populating of the coastal valleys proceeded apace throughout the Early Horizon but, by the end of the period, different valleys had very different population densities. Thus, for example, all parts of the Ica Valley on the south coast contain numerous late Early Horizon sites. In contrast, only a handful of relatively insignificant Early Horizon sites are known in the Chillón Valley of the central coast or in the Virú Valley of the north coast, despite the fact that these valleys have been surveyed as extensively as has Ica. We lack data on the productivity of fishing in each of these zones, but in all probability the speed with which a valley was occupied and with which its population multiplied was a function of the opportunities offered by the coastal fishing stations. In an area with many productive beaches, bays, and rocky points, we might expect that many new settlements would be established on the shore, and that the valleys would be settled only slowly until the shore stations were all inhabited. In contrast, a rapidly expanding population in a zone with limited fishing possibilities would be obliged to exploit the valleys more quickly and more intensively. This difference of marine productivity explains the differential rate of valley occupation between the Ica and Chillón Valleys. Whether or not it is a universally valid explanation remains to be explored in the future.

The north-central coast, which had a head start in the population race, seems to have had a dense valley population during the Early Horizon. Interestingly, it is in this region that we find the earliest dated fortress in ancient Peru. The hilltop redoubt of Chanquillo in the Casma Valley has a radiocarbon date of 342 ± 80 B.C. This date was run on a sample of wood from a lintel beam, and should represent the time of construction of the fortress. As we shall see (see p. 120), the evidence of intensive warfare in ancient Peru coincided with the expansion of population to the limits of the food-production potential of the land. Though it is not possible to estimate the Early Horizon population of the Casma Valley, the construction of the Chanquillo fortress probably represents the first step in this process.

We can safely assume that the coastal peoples of the Early Horizon dug and used at least small irrigation ditches. So far as this writer knows, none of the major ancient irrigation systems can be dated earlier than the beginning of the Early Intermediate Period. It is possible, nevertheless, that some of them were constructed during the Early Horizon. There is nothing more difficult to date than an irrigation system or ditch. Most of the ancient systems are still in use, hence are not available for excavation. Some abandoned ditches are known, but few or none of them have been excavated. Since ditches were cleaned every year, even extensive excavations might not produce specimens dating to the time of their construction. At present, we can date the digging of a ditch or canal only when it is directly associated with a settlement of known age. Under the circumstances, all that we can say is that many major irrigation systems were in use during the Early Intermediate Period but that the construction of some of them may have been started during the Early Horizon. Similarly, agricultural terraces in the highlands have gone almost unstudied. It is doubtful though, if any of them were built as early as the Early Horizon. Unlike the coastal irrigation systems, which multiplied agricultural land many times over, the highlands hillside terraces added only minor amounts of farmland. Given the small number of Early Horizon sites yet known in the highlands, it seems most unlikely that the fertile bottom lands were all under cultivation, and there seems to be no reason why hillside terraces should be built as long as good bottom land was yet available.

Perhaps the most important development of the Early Horizon was the growth of large towns or small cities. We have already mentioned Chavín de Huántar as an urban town or possibly even a synchoritic city (see p. 103). John H. Rowe has described two large sites in the Ica Valley as follows:

> . . . Media Luna is an area of continuous, concentrated habitation refuse over a kilometer across, with fifteen small adobe mounds and some remains of adobe walls on the flat. The mounds presumably represent temples or other public buildings. There are no fortifications at this site. The Tajahuana site is only slightly smaller. The whole area is covered with stones representing the foundations of small rectangular houses, and there are a number of mounds about the same size as the ones at Media Luna. Tajahuana is elaborately fortified with multiple walls and a dry moat on the side of easiest access.
>
> Both of the sites described were occupied only . . . for a century or a century and a half, and then never occupied again. They apparently represent achoritic cities, without smaller settlements between them, but we have no evidence of their economic life . . . .
>
> There is no indication that the urban settlements . . . depended in any way on large scale irrigation works.[7]

Judging by their size and density, both of these sites were probably large enough to be called cities. In spite of their achorism, they must be viewed as the precursors of the great cities that grew up in southern Peru during the Early Intermediate Period.

TECHNOLOGICAL ADVANCES

Metallurgy, the last of the arts to be developed in ancient Peru, made its appearance during the Early Horizon. Small beads of copper and gold have been found at Chiripa in Bolivia. Copper was used for spearthrower hooks and small ornaments near the

[7] Rowe, "Urban Settlements," p. 9.

end of the Early Horizon on the south coast. From the north, many beautiful objects of gold in Chavín style have come from the Lambayeque Valley, and some are also said to have come from Chavín de Huántar.[8] Whereas the southern copper was worked only by cold hammering and annealing, the northern gold work already shows considerable sophistication of technique. Thin sheets were cut, embossed, or hammered over molds (repoussé), and were joined by welding and soldering. Ear spools, nose ornaments, pectorals, plaques, and crowns bore the classical figures of Chavín mythology. Most of these pieces date from late in the Early Horizon, but a few of them may have been made in quite early Chavín times. It seems apparent from present evidence that ancient Andean gold metallurgy originated somewhere in the northern Andes— northern Peru, Ecuador, or perhaps Colombia. Copper smithing, on the other hand, was a southern invention. Its origins may have been in southern Peru, western Bolivia, northwestern Argentina, or northern Chile—an area which includes most of the copper deposits in South America.

Technical proficiency also advanced in other media. The most spectacular developments were in the field of textiles. After the simple beginnings of the heddle loom in the Initial Period, the Early Horizon saw a growing artistry in a profusion of styles and techniques. Gauze, tapestry, painted cloth, double cloth, embroidery, and pattern weaves were all being made on the coast before the period ended. The basic loom was not essentially different from that used by Andean weavers today. It is called a *backstrap loom* and consists of two rods with the warps stretched between them. One rod is suspended from a firm support; the other is attached to a belt around the weaver's back. Shed rods, heddles, and battens all consisted of differently shaped sticks set in the stretched warps. By leaning backward or forward the weaver could control the tension of the warps at will. The backstrap loom does not permit the manufacture of cloth much over a yard wide. In later periods wide cloths were made on stationary frame looms. It is not known whether such large looms were in use during the Early Horizon.

[8] Samuel K. Lothrop, "Gold Artifacts in Chavín Style," American Antiquity, XVI, No. 3 (1951), 226-27.

VIII

The Rise of Cities

As we have seen, Preceramic Period VI was a time of rapid, fundamental culture change. The Initial Period continued and intensified the new ways of life initiated during late preceramic times. In a sense, the spread of the Chavín cult can be seen as the culmination of these earlier trends. The Early Intermediate Period, beginning about 200 B.C., was again a time of revolutionary change. The first really large cities were built at this time, and some of them served as the capitals of fairly large regional states. Most of the valley-wide irrigation systems of the coast were built during the Early Intermediate Period. For the first time, intensive warfare became a factor in the everyday life of the ancient Peruvians. Fortresses and fortified towns and cities sprang up all across ancient Peru. Population, which had been expanding steadily since late preceramic times, now reached its maximum size in many parts of Peru. Art and technology reached their peak on the coast at this time, and some of the finest masterpieces in the history of art date from the Early Intermediate Period.

Since many of the fundamental changes that took place during the Early Intermediate Period were related to the large size of the population, we will look first at the problem of estimating popula-

112

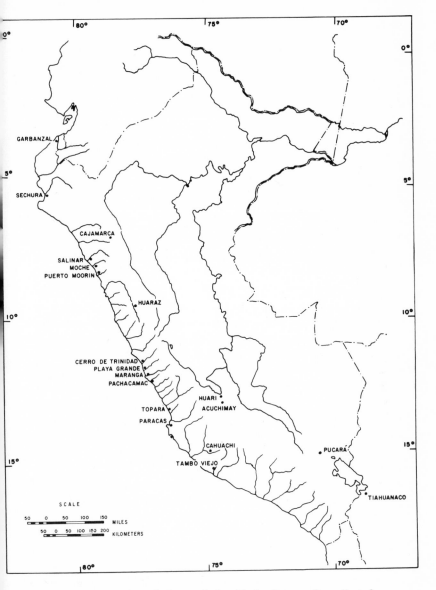

MAP 6. Archaeological Sites of the Early Intermediate Period

tion density and distribution. The archaeological evidence does not permit an accurate estimate of the size of the Central Andean population, but it was certainly many times greater than that of the Preceramic Stage or the Initial Period. Judging by the number and size of archaeological sites, many of the coastal valleys reached their maximum population before the beginning of the Middle Horizon. The highlands basins seem not to have been so thickly peopled as in later times, but the total population of the highlands must have been at least half of the number that the Spaniards found there in 1532. Curiously, however, some regions appear to have suffered a partial depopulation. The north-central coast, which was the most thickly populated part of the country during Period VI and the Initial Period, was the most prominent case of this type. Whereas the first half of the Early Intermediate Period is represented by many archaeological sites in this region, habitations of the late Early Intermediate Period are almost impossible to find. Donald E. Thompson has summarized the problem with relation to one north-central coastal valley:

There is . . . very little evidence at present that the Casma Valley was even occupied during the period of regional florescence [latter part of the Early Intermediate Period] . . . .

. . . present evidence suggests either that the valley was abandoned for a considerable time or that, if there were inhabitants during this period, they preserved only a simple rural culture, receiving little if any stimulus from their neighbors to the north and south. . . . it seems preferable to assume that there were some inhabitants during this period. Such a population, if it were scattered over the valley floor in perishable dwellings, would leave little outward trace of its existence after so many centuries of intensive cultivation.

The singular lack of any positively dated "classic" [late Early Intermediate Period] sites leads the author to tend to favor the proposition that all the . . . pyramids belong to the formative period [Early Horizon and early Early Intermediate Period] and that the "classic" in Casma consisted merely of a small rural population which was scattered over the valley floor and produced no monumental architecture.[1]

[1] Donald E. Thompson, "The Problem of Dating Certain Stone-faced Stepped Pyramids on the North Coast of Peru," *Southwestern Journal of Anthropology*, XVIII, No. 4 (1962), 298-99.

It has been estimated that the population of the Inca Empire at the time of its discovery by the Spaniards in the sixteenth century was approximately six million.[2] Since the population at the end of the Early Intermediate Period must have been well over half of the sixteenth century figure, we may estimate some four to four and a half million persons, of whom at least three million lived in Peru proper. Whereas in the sixteenth century perhaps less than half of the population lived on the coast, during the Early Intermediate Period there were probably more people living on the Peruvian coast than in all the rest of the Central Andes. This gives us about two million coastal dwellers, as contrasted to our late preceramic estimate of 50,000.

Many of the revolutionary changes of the Early Intermediate Period can be traced directly to the increased population. Irrigation systems, cities, fortresses, and conquest states can be seen as responses to the need for feeding, housing, and defending large numbers of people and for satisfying their need for living space.

URBANISM

The trend toward large settlements which was evident at Chavín de Huántar and in the Ica Valley during the Early Horizon culminated during the Early Intermediate Period in the building of some of the largest of the ancient cities of Peru. Three great cities of this time are known in the southern highlands, together with several smaller ones. The large cities are Tiahuanaco in the southern Titicaca basin, Pucara in the northern Titicaca basin and Huari in the upper Mantaro region. Each city consisted of a nucleus of monumental public buildings and plazas, together with extensive residential districts, the whole covering from one to four square miles. Each was the focal point of a synchoritic system which also included rural and urban towns and numerous villages. Any or all of the three major cities may have had populations in excess of ten thousand persons.

Neither Huari nor Pucara has been adequately described in the

[2] John H. Rowe, "Inca Culture at the Time of the Spanish Conquest," in *Handbook of South American Indians,* ed. Julian H. Steward, Bureau of American Ethnology, Bulletin 143, II (Washington, D.C.: Smithsonian Institution, 1946), 184-85.

literature, but both clearly conformed to the pattern of large, nucleated, synchoritic cities. Pucara was occupied for only a brief period, perhaps no more than 200 years, at the beginning of the Early Intermediate Period. Huari seems to have been built somewhat later and was occupied through the latter part of the period and most of the Middle Horizon. It is not known whether most of the visible ruins at Huari date to the Early Intermediate Period or to the Middle Horizon, but Early Intermediate refuse covers the entire enormous area of the city. There is no question that, during the Early Intermediate Period, it was a great metropolitan center. Both Huari and Pucara, like Tiahuanaco, are famed for their stone statues and stelae. Some of the statues were carved during the Middle Horizon, but others—including all of those at Pucara— were of Early Intermediate Period manufacture.

Near the modern city of Ayacucho, not far from Huari, there were three smaller cities called Chakipampa, Acuchimay, and Ñawimpukyu, which were to achieve considerable prominence at the beginning of the Middle Horizon. Late in the Early Intermediate Period they were probably linked economically to Huari, though the political relationships of the time cannot be traced.

Tiahuanaco is one of the most famous ruins in all of the Central Andes. It is usually described as a ceremonial center, but extensive refuse deposits have been reported there. Its fame as a ceremonial center is probably due to the fact that all of the excavations at Tiahuanaco have been conducted in the nucleus of the city. The nuclear buildings included a large stone-faced platform mound, large platforms with sunken courtyards in the middle, a semisubterranean temple, and a "palace." These buildings are famous for the perfection of their dressed stone masonry and for the use of copper cramps to join the blocks of stone. Most of them were built late in the Early Intermediate Period, though the platform mound may be of Middle Horizon date. The extent of the habitation refuse surrounding this central area has never been determined.

Somewhat smaller cities also grew up on the south coast during the Early Intermediate Period. During the century or two before Christ, there was a city in each of the Pisco, Ica, Nazca, and Acarí Valleys. Urban life may not have lasted long in some of these valleys, but there was at least one city in the Ica Valley at any given time throughout the Early Intermediate Period. Each of these south coastal settlements consisted of densely packed houses with field stone foundations together with several open plazas. At Cahuachi in the Nazca Valley, there was also a central pyramid. Tambo Viejo in the Acarí Valley was surrounded by a fortification wall of stones and adobes. Each of these south coastal cities was probably the center of a synchoritic system that included a large part of its respective valley. Only Cahuachi, however, shows the nucleated pattern typical of the great synchoritic cities of the highlands.

In contrast to the urbanization of the south, the old pattern of scattered population and ceremonial centers continued all across the northern half of Peru. Tremendous numbers of large, elegant pyramids and platform mounds were built in this area, almost all of them dating to the latter part of the Early Intermediate Period. These structures were all made of adobes, usually quite small ones, and they frequently had elaborate mural paintings. Sometimes six or eight pyramids were clustered together in a single ceremonial center. Perhaps the most famous of these ceremonial centers are that of Maranga in the city of Lima and that represented by the "Pyramid of the Sun" and the "Pyramid of the Moon" in the Moche Valley. Though none of these centers had significant resident populations, an enormous amount of time and energy went into making the billions of adobe bricks and assembling the pyramids. We can get an idea of the size of the undertaking when we realize that, before the recent expansion of the city of Lima, there were between fifty and one hundred major pyramids in the lower Rimac Valley alone.

Together with the multiplication of ceremonial centers, we find a shift from separate villages to the dispersed community pattern. This process did not take place at the same rate in all valleys and may never have happened in some of them. It certainly occurred during the Early Intermediate Period in the Chillón and Virú Valleys—the two most intensively studied valleys of the central and north coast. Dispersed settlements were a way of maximizing farm land, and were related to the topography of the coastal valleys and to the large populations that needed to be fed. They were built on infertile alluvial cones along the edges of the valleys in order to leave the bottom lands free for cultivation. The size of each group of houses depended on the size of the alluvial cone on which it was built. Typically, the settlement units were spread out along the edges of the valleys in irregular lines, the spacing between units depending on the distance between alluvial cones. The space between houses on each cone varied considerably, depending on local tradition. There is usually no way of determining where one community ended and the next began or whether, perhaps, all of the communities in a single small valley represented a single sociopolitical unit.

The north coast, the north-central coast (insofar as Early Intermediate sites are known there), and the northern highlands seem to have been entirely organized on the basis of ceremonial centers and either dispersed communities or numerous villages. The same arrangement was also dominant on the central coast, but the latter region also saw the development of at least one large urban town or small city. This settlement was Cerro de Trinidad in the lower Chancay Valley. The site consists of a large isolated hill near the sea which is surrounded by habitation refuse and house foundations, and which has a number of temple structures and a large stone-walled enclosure on its lower flanks (Plate 3). Other large settlements, each of which may have had several thousand residents, were Playa Grande on the shore north of the Chillón Valley and Cerro Culebra in the lower Chillón Valley. At each of these sites one or more temples formed a nucleus for the settlement. There were also Early Intermediate settlements at Cajamarquilla (Rimac Valley) and Pachacamac (Lurín Valley), both of which grew into cities in later times. It is doubtful, however, whether during the Early Intermediate Period Pachacamac was more than a ceremonial center or Cajamarquilla more than a village.

The organization of the northern populations—into dispersed communities focused on the ceremonial centers—obviously served the same functions as the urban organization of the south. Both were ways of housing large numbers of people without usurping much-needed farm land, and both were organizations which provided for efficient distribution of food, services, and other goods. The ceremonial center pattern has aptly been called "civilization without cities." It represented a different distribution of people and of such functions as markets and craft centers, but it was probably as efficient as urbanism in assuring the survival and prosperity of its people.

PLATE 3. Part of an Adobe Temple Structure at Cerro de Trinidad, Chancay Valley (*Photo by Ernesto Tabio*)

The south coastal cities and the northern ceremonial centers occupied essentially the same environment and operated on the same economic base. With the addition of the potato, which was now frequently illustrated on pottery vessels, the basic coastal crop list was complete. Maize, squash, beans, manioc, *achira*, *lúcuma*, and chili peppers were the basis of coastal life; fish and guinea pigs provided proteins; extensive acreage was dedicated to cotton: and the llama was raised for its wool. Major irrigation systems, controlling essentially all of the water of the coastal rivers, were built in each valley at this time. Some of them may have been begun during the Early Horizon, but none can yet be surely dated before the beginning of the Early Intermediate Period. They were not, however, all built at the same time. Thus, for example, a large system in the upper Chancay Valley was constructed at the very beginning of the Early Intermediate Period, whereas the

Virú system dates to about the time of Christ or shortly thereafter, and that of the Ica Valley was not built until near the end of the period.

There can be no doubt that the political unification of each valley was now complete. For although it might have been possible to dig the irrigation ditches through a system of intercommunity cooperation, the annual cleaning of the ditches and the equitable distribution of water could only have been accomplished by an over-all authority capable of dictating the destinies of all of the dwellers in a valley.

The shore fishermen continued to live in villages, as they have ever since. However, these villages were now definitely an integral part of the larger society and were maintained primarily to supply proteins to the valleys. The construction of fish-drying terraces at Ancón and Ventanilla, and probably on many other parts of the coast, indicates that fishing was now industrialized and was functioning only as part of the mixed agricultural economy. The importance of fishing to this economy is indicated by the fact that some of the fishing villages, such as Playa Grande, were protected by hilltop fortresses like those which also appeared in the valleys at this time.

Life in the highlands undoubtedly depended on agriculture. For most of the area there is no way of estimating the relative importance of maize and of the Andean root crops. Maize cannot have been important in the Titicaca Basin, which was too high for its effective cultivation. Pucara and Tiahuanaco, which lie above 12,000 feet altitude, must have depended on potatoes, *quinoa, oca, ulluco,* llamas, alpacas, and guinea pigs.

WARFARE AND CONQUEST

Cities and dispersed communities served to house large populations without encroaching on farm lands. Irrigation systems were built to extend the arable land in order to feed many mouths. Still another effect of this ancient population explosion was the increase in intensive warfare and conquest as a means of extending the boundaries of administrative units. The prevalence of warfare at this time is abundantly clear in the archaeological record. Every coastal valley that has been well surveyed has turned out to have fortresses and fortified settlements dating to the Early Intermediate Period. Weapons are abundant in archaeological sites, particularly on the south coast. Representations of warriors, battle scenes, and trophy heads, formerly rare, now became an obsession of coastal artists. Trophy heads are often found in graves of this time, and many mummies show signs of death by violence. Although there is little evidence from the highlands because of the small amount of research that has been done there, warfare was probably as prevalent there as it was on the coast.

It is also apparent that much of the warfare consisted of more than simple reciprocal raiding, and that there was now more at stake than the superiority of one's gods. Evidence has been cited to show that the people of Moche and Chicama conquered the north coastal valleys as far south as Virú, Santa, and Nepeña, and that the people of Nazca conquered the Acarí Valley.[3] In each case, the ensuing uniformity of style and culture is adequate to allow the inference that the conquered peoples were incorporated into the Moche and Nazca states, rather than simply looted. Judging by the distribution of ceramic styles, there was also a Topará state in the Cañete, Chincha, and Pisco Valleys early in the period, and a Lima state in the Rimac, Chillón, and Chancay Valleys. Highlands states, too, may have been more extensive than in earlier times, but we lack the evidence needed to trace their boundaries.

It is highly significant that war and conquest became endemic just at the time when cities, dispersed communities, irrigation systems, and large valley populations appeared in the archaeological record. It is doubtful that warfare functioned to limit population in a Malthusian sense. Certainly many young men of breeding age died in battle—their headless bodies are all too common in cemeteries. But the enlarged states, once established, provided peaceful areas within which normal population growth could continue unimpeded. The significance of the timing mentioned above is rather that it demonstrates that the causes of war were funda-

[3] William Duncan Strong and Clifford Evans, Jr., *Cultural Stratigraphy in the Virú Valley, Northern Peru.* Columbia Studies in Archaeology and Ethnology, IV (New York: Columbia University Press, 1952), 216-18; Rowe, "Urban Settlements," p. 11.

mental economic ones. As long as there was plenty of fertile land available, evidence of bloodshed was rare; once there were too many people on the land, conquest, along with irrigation and special settlement patterns, came into play as means of acquiring new acreage.

ARTISTS, GODS, AND MEN

The Moche and Nazca Cultures of the Early Intermediate Period are famous for the beauty and elegance of their art work. Fine specimens are sought by collectors and prized by museums of art and archaeology. The masterpieces of Moche art were done in pottery, especially in the form of stirrup spout bottles. Moche figure painting rivaled that of the ancient Greeks, and certain modeled portrait heads are among the world's finest sculpture. Nazca art, less realistic than that of Moche, is noted for its polychromy. Pottery bottles and bowls and embroidered textiles commonly employ seven or eight colors and sometimes more in subtle and elegant combinations (Plates 4 and 5).

The most spectacular single find ever made in Peru was the so-called *Paracas Necropolis*. This "necropolis," excavated by Julio C. Tello in 1929, consisted of a cache of 429 mummies piled up in an abandoned house on the Paracas Peninsula. As always, the mummies were wrapped in many layers of cloth and were accompanied by foodstuffs, pottery vessels, and other grave goods. Most of them date to the first phase of the Nazca Culture, at the beginning of the Early Intermediate Period. What makes the find so spectacular is the great number of beautiful embroidered mantles, shirts, skirts, turbans, and other cloths. Any museum would consider itself fortunate to own so much as one polychrome cloth from the Paracas Necropolis.

The archaeologist values a Moche figure painting or clay sculpture, a Nazca embroidery or painted bottle, for more than its beauty. Moche and Nazca artists, more than any others in ancient Peru, portrayed the figures and scenes of everyday life and of their mythology. They have left us their own view of the world in which they lived. By combining these representations with the evidence of public and domestic architecture, of settlement patterns, and of

PLATE 4. Moche Bottle Showing a Criminal Punished by Being Exposed to Vultures (*Courtesy of the Museum of Primitive Art*)

plant and animal remains, we can get a remarkably complete picture of life on the coast in the Early Intermediate Period.

The artists had an extraordinary interest in plants and animals, both wild and domestic. Moche potters portrayed at least thirty-five different species of birds, sixteen of mammals, and sixteen of fish, as well as a great variety of other animals. Pumas, condors, parrots,

PLATE 5. Nazca "Sampler" on which Polychrome Embroidered Designs Were Laid out before Being Transferred to the Final Product (*Courtesy of the Museum of Primitive Art*)

and spotted cats may have been seen by the artists in the upper coastal valleys, but the monkeys so common in Nazca art can only have been imported from the *montaña*. There are many Moche scenes showing deer being hunted with the spearthrower and club. Moche fishermen put to sea in one-man canoes made of bundles of *totora* rushes, while the Nazca fisherman rode an inflated skin that he paddled with his hands. A Moche bottle shows a man hunting birds with a blowgun, a weapon which must have been introduced from the tropical forest. Nearly the whole range of coastal crops are illustrated, as are digging sticks and possibly other farm tools. One delightful Nazca painted cloth shows birds raiding the garden and making off with maize, squash, *pepino*, chili peppers, and other fruits. The farmer's vexations are also made clear on a few Nazca pottery vessels which portray mice eating the ears of maize off the plant.

The scenes and characters of daily life are common on Moche pottery. We recognize the hunter, the soldier, the weaver, the beggar, the disabled veteran, the prisoner of war, the mother with her baby, the messenger, the governor, and all of the other people to be seen on the streets of a busy town. One remarkable Moche specimen shows a textile factory, with several weavers working under the supervision of a foreman. Other scenes show battles or the bringing home of naked prisoners with ropes around their necks. Government officials are shown carried in litters or seated on thrones and receiving messengers or delegations. Every rank and class seems to have had its own distinctive dress patterns, hairdos, hats, and ornaments. Nazca artists had less interest in portraying their fellow men, but fishermen, warriors, and musicians are illustrated. Especially delightful is the occasional Nazca representation of a one-man band—a seated figure playing a pottery panpipe with his mouth, a pottery trumpet with his ear, and shaking a gourd rattle held in his trumpet hand, while he holds a pottery drum on his knee and is sometimes shown using his penis as a drumstick.

Both Nazca and Moche artists have left us a visual record of their deities and myths. Nazca deities and mythological beings may take the shape of men, birds, or killer whales. They were inevitably associated with trophy heads and often carried the semicircular knives used for taking heads. Moche deities, too, are often shown with trophy heads and semicircular knives, but they appear in many other contexts as well. The principal Moche deity, the *Tusked God,* appears as hunter, soldier, fisherman, maize or manioc plant, crab, or in other forms. In all of his incarnations except the agricultural ones he often does battle with a fin-backed adversary. He may be shown as a supreme ruler seated on a throne and being served by his subjects. Lesser beings include such figures as bird warriors and animated weapons. Just as trophy heads were ubiquitous in Nazca mythology, so also the theme of war runs throughout the art work of Moche. Gods do battle, the weapons revolt, prisoners and trophy heads are taken in the supernatural world as they were in the world of men.

Moche metallurgy was also particularly sophisticated. Most Early Intermediate Period metal work was simply a continuation of Early Horizon techniques and materials with the addition of gold-copper alloys and, late in the period, of simple casting. Except for spearthrower hooks, tweezers, and fishhooks, copper and gold were dedicated to the production of ornaments. Moche smiths also used silver, silver-copper and gold-silver-copper alloys. They used not only the old techniques of hammering, annealing, cutting, embossing, repoussé, and soldering, but also turquoise mosaic inlay, gilding, simple casting, and "lost wax" casting, in which a hollow cast was produced by letting the molten metal replace a wax lining in the mold. The Moche metal workers also smelted copper in ceramic crucibles and cast it into ingots of various shapes for storage. Besides ornaments, which were mostly of gold and the various alloys, they made copper chisels, spear points, and digging stick points.

On the whole, the picture we get of coastal life at this time is one of an intensely specialized and stratified society with well-defined ranks and professions symbolized by details of dress and ornament. There were rulers and ruled, soldiers and civilians, farmers and city people, priests and laymen, craftsmen, merchants and customers, beggars and—undoubtedly—thieves. We have come a long way from the simple village society of late preceramic times.

IX

The First Round
of Empire

The Middle Horizon, beginning about A.D. 600, saw the rise
and fall of two great empires with their capitals at Huari and
Tiahuanaco. The Huari Empire, at its greatest extent, included all
of the coast and highlands from Chicama and Cajamarca in the
north to Ocoña and Sicuani in the south, with the possible exception of the central coast. The Tiahuanaco people conquered
the whole of the Titicaca Basin, all of Peru south of the Majes
Valley and Arequipa, and the coast and highlands of northern
Chile (Map 8). Neither empire lasted more than a century or two
but, during this brief span, there was an interchange of goods and
ideas across the Central Andes such as had never been seen
before. Though regional styles and cultures would again emerge,
the Huari and Tiahuanaco conquests put an end to the old regional
isolation. Never again would the ancient Peruvians live in ignorance
of the country beyond the nearest valley or two.

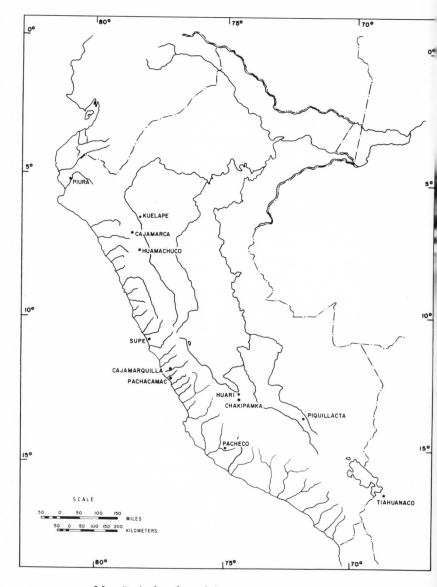

MAP 7. Archaeological Sites of the Middle Horizon

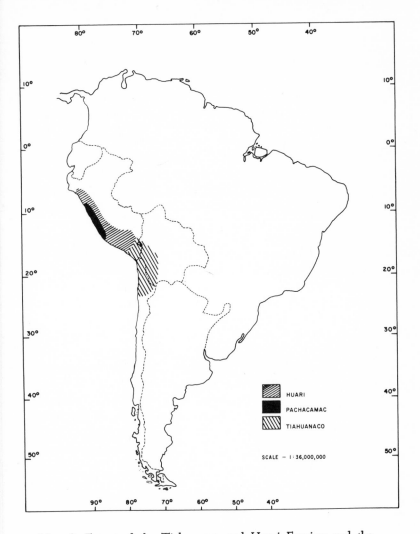

MAP 8. Extent of the Tiahuanaco and Huari Empires and the Pachacamac Sphere of Influence

THE TIAHUANACO EMPIRE

The story of the Middle Horizon begins at Tiahuanaco in the southern Titicaca Basin. This ancient city, located at an altitude of 12,750 feet, was occupied throughout the Early Intermediate Period (see p. 116). Most of the monumental structures comprising the nucleus of the city were probably built before A.D. 600, but a great platform mound known as *Acapana* may have been built at the beginning of the Middle Horizon. At this time, too, many new stone carvings were erected, including the famous "Gateway of the Sun." This gate (which need not have had anything to do with the sun) is carved of a single large block of stone and portrays the principal Tiahuanaco deity flanked by rows of winged "angels." The deity, whom we may call the *Gateway God,* is shown front-face with a feline mouth, grasping staves or scepters in both hands. He is so similar in concept and associations to the old Chavín Staff God that he is very likely a later representation of the same deity. Why he should appear at Tiahuanaco, outside the area of Chavín influence and nearly a millennium after the extinction of the Chavín cult, is a mystery that remains unsolved. There are some hints, though, that the Chavín cult may not have died out completely at the end of the Early Horizon. Chavín feline designs were revived from time to time on Moche pots of the Early Intermediate Period, and one fine Chavín revival piece has been reported from the Middle Horizon at Vista Alegre in the Rimac Valley. The temple walls at Chavín de Huántar were ornamented with carved stone tenon heads. Heads of this sort were rare in ancient Peru, and the fact that they were also used during the Early Intermediate Period in the Callejón de Huaylas and at Tiahuanaco again suggests some continuation of the Chavín mythology. Though there is no proof of what happened, it is fascinating to speculate that the Chavín cult survived as a minority religion and that it again took root— after a long time and a great deal of stylistic change—far to the south of its original homeland.

Whatever the history of the Staff/Gateway God, we again find him at the head of one of the great unifying movements of Peruvian prehistory. At some time around the beginning of the Middle Horizon, objects in Tiahuanaco style, usually depicting the Gateway God, his attendant "angels," or the feline and eagle figures so common in Tiahuanaco art, began to appear in the northern Titicaca Basin, in the southernmost highlands and on the far south coast of Peru, and in northern Chile as far south as the Río Loa in the Atacama Desert (Plate 6). These "pure" Tiahuanaco

PLATE 6. Tiahuanaco Beaker with Feline Head and Drinking Tube (*Courtesy of the Museum of Primitive Art*)

pieces existed side by side—at least in some regions—with specimens in local styles, some of which showed varying degrees of Tiahuanaco influence.

Unfortunately, the only Middle Horizon sites in all of this territory that have ever been studied in detail are Tiahuanaco itself and a couple of smaller temples in its immediate vicinity. We cannot, therefore, say much about the nature of the Tiahuanaco expansion except to indicate that it happened quickly, probably early in the Middle Horizon, and that the period of unification was finished by the end of the Middle Horizon. Indeed, were it not for the relationship of the Tiahuanaco expansion to the conquest of the Huari Empire (see below), it would be impossible to decide whether we were dealing with an empire or with an expansive cult like that of Chavín. Given the relationship and the evidence that the Huari expansion was a matter of conquest, it is probably safe to assume that the far-flung finds of Tiahuanaco specimens reflect the marching of Tiahuanaco armies and the establishment of Tiahuanaco governors in the provinces of a greatly expanded Tiahuanaco state.

The only city yet known in this broad territory is Tiahuanaco itself, and the only temples are in the same region of the southern Titicaca Basin. It would be unwise, however, to conclude that urban and ceremonial patterns were restricted to the area around the capital. So little is known of the Middle Horizon elsewhere in Tiahuanaco territory that any number of large cities and ceremonial sites may yet lie undiscovered.

THE HUARI EMPIRE

Much more archaeological research has been done in Huari territory, and a thorough study by Dorothy Menzel has done much to elucidate the nature and timing of the Huari expansion. Her long article on the Middle Horizon chronology of the Montara Basin and of the south and central coast has revealed much about the way in which the city of Huari was transformed into the capital of an empire that encompassed almost all of Peru.[1]

Menzel divides the Middle Horizon into four "epochs," the first two of which are in turn subdivided into two parts. With a total span of some 400 years for the Middle Horizon, one may guess that each epoch lasted about a century.

Late in the Early Intermediate Period there was close contact between the southern Mantaro Basin and the south coastal valleys

[1] Dorothy Menzel, "Style and Time in the Middle Horizon," Ñawpa Pacha, II (1964), 1-105.

of Ica and Nazca, the cultures of the latter having had a particularly strong influence on that of the Mantaro region. Tiahuanaco entered into this exchange at the beginning of the Middle Horizon in a very special way. During Epoch 1A (ca. A.D. 600-650) the town of Chakipampa near Ayacucho evidently became an important ceremonial site. Large polychrome urns of a purely ceremonial nature were made there and were "sacrificed" in rituals in which large numbers of them were broken. These urns carried designs taken from the stone sculptures at Tiahuanaco, including both the Gateway God and his angels. Since evidence for conquest is lacking in Epoch 1A, Menzel suggests that the Tiahuanaco religion was brought "either by missionaries from the Tiahuanaco center or by men from the area of Ayacucho and Huari who learned the new religion abroad and brought it home." [2]

Epoch 1B (ca. A.D. 650-700) saw the first expansion of the Huari state. There were now three centers at which the ceremonial urns were being made and sacrificed, including not only Chakipampa but also the city of Huari itself and the site of Pacheco in the Nazca Valley. The latter seems actually to have been a settlement of highlanders on the coast, since a large part of the ordinary pottery at the site is in the style of the southern Mantaro Basin rather than that of the south coast. Trade pieces and imitations of the same style have also been found throughout the Mantaro drainage, in the Callejón de Huaylas, and along the whole of the central and south coast. This pottery, known as *Chakipampa B*, made use of some motifs of the ceremonial urns but did not yet portray the mythological figures themselves. Since no Chakipampa B pottery is known from the Titicaca Basin, it is evident that this was a separate expansion independent of that of Tiahuanaco. Its distribution, primarily in ceremonial centers, cities, and other high-prestige sites, is much the same as that of the later Inca pottery, and provides one kind of evidence that the Huari expansion was based on conquest like that of the later Incas.

Epoch 2A (ca. A.D. 700-750) saw the abandonment of Chakipampa and the other cities in the vicinity of Ayacucho and the emergence of Huari as the exclusive capital of the new empire. Perhaps the conquest was carried out by an unstable federation of

[2] *Ibid.*, p. 67.

cities in the Mantaro Basin, which finally resolved their conflicts by force. The boundaries of the empire were not further expanded during Epoch 2A, but its consolidation proceeded apace. Huari and Huari-derived pottery styles were now being made in abundance throughout the empire, and the local styles began to lose importance. The Huari style of Epoch 2 is known as *Viñaque*. It was a spectacular polychrome ware that made extensive use of the Tiahuanacoid mythological figures, including the Gateway God, angels, felines, and eagles, sometimes fully represented and sometimes in abbreviated forms. New polychrome pottery styles also grew up in the Nazca Valley and on the central coast, each style combining Viñaque vessel shapes and designs with older local stylistic features. The Atarco style of Nazca seems to have been particularly important, since it included some designs from both Tiahuanaco and Epoch 1 ceremonial urns that were never made on ordinary pottery at Huari, and since it seems to have been extensively traded around the south coast.

During Epoch 2B (ca. A.D. 750-800) the Huari Empire again expanded, this time northward to Cajamarca and the Chicama Valley and southward nearly to the Titicaca Basin and to the Ocoña Valley on the coast. Though no Huari specimens have ever been found in Ecuador, there is some evidence for the interchange of stylistic ideas northward beyond the borders of empire. The Tunchaván D and Elen Pata styles of the southern Ecuadorean highlands include vessel shapes and drinking tubes derived from Viñaque, whereas the widespread use of tripod vessel supports in the northern half of Peru during Epoch 2 may represent Ecuadorean influence. To the south there seems to have been little or no contact between the Huari and Tiahuanaco empires.

Widespread evidence attests to the military nature of the Huari expansion. Viñaque pottery was exported across the whole empire, and high prestige provincial styles, such as that of Cajamarca III, were imported to the capital. Viñaque imitations and Viñaque-inspired local polychrome styles were made everywhere, while many of the older regional stylistic traditions were rapidly disappearing. In the words of Wendell C. Bennett, "That the . . . expansion was made possible through strong military support is implied from the evidence of strong disruption of the local cultures . . . ." [3] Building complexes in pure Huari architectural style, representing government storehouses, army barracks, or both, were constructed at Piquillacta in the Apurimac Valley and at Viracochapampa near Huamachuco. Throughout the provinces, the fanciest of the Huari-influenced polychrome pottery was concentrated in the cemeteries of the well-to-do, indicating that the local nobility of the Middle Horizon, like their descendants in Inca times, adopted the manners of their conquerors. If we cannot yet identify many Huari administrative centers in the provinces, it is only because so little excavation has been done in Middle Horizon sites.

At the end of Epoch 2 the empire disintegrated and the city of Huari was abandoned. Before inquiring into the fall of the empire, though, we must look more closely at some of the events in the provinces during Epochs 1 and 2.

PACHACAMAC

The settlement of Pachacamac on the central coast seems to have enjoyed a very special status within the Huari empire. Pachacamac had been a ceremonial center during the Early Intermediate Period. During the Middle Horizon it grew into a major city. Excavations at Pachacamac have not been adequate to date the process of growth in detail, so that we cannot say, "at this time it was still a ceremonial center," and "at that time it had become a city." It reached its maximum growth during the Late Intermediate Period, after a period of expansion that must have lasted throughout the Middle Horizon.

A new art style was created at Pachacamac during Epoch 2, and it spread over a large part of the coast. The new style, which is best represented on pottery and in polychrome tapestries, was a Tiahuanacoid style related to Viñaque and Atarco but specializing in the portrayal of eagle designs. During Epoch 2B, when the Pachacamac style was at its apogee, it dominated the central coast almost to the exclusion of the Viñaque style. Pachacamac designs

[3] Wendell C. Bennett, *Excavations at Wari, Ayacucho, Peru,* Yale University Publications in Anthropology, IL (New Haven: Yale University Press, 1953), 117.

were copied as far south as Ica and Nazca and as far north as the Chicama Valley, and may even have influenced the Viñaque style of Huari itself (Plate 7). In general, the further one goes from

PLATE 7. Cup Showing Pachacamac Stylistic Influence (*Courtesy of the Museum of Primitive Art*)

the city of Pachacamac the less "pure" are the specimens found until, when one reaches Chicama, one finds that Viñaque and Pachacamac designs were combined on individual pottery vessels. In short, Pachacamac enjoyed great prestige at this time, but the "pure" Pachacamac style does not show the distribution typical of imperial styles, and there is no reason to assume that there was a Pachacamac empire equivalent to those of Huari and Tiahuanaco.

In later times, there was a famous oracle at Pachacamac. The Incas, when they conquered the coast, showed great respect for the oracle, traveled great distances to consult it, and gave its priests an unprecedented measure of independence. The best explanation for the high prestige of Pachacamac during the Middle Horizon is the suggestion that the oracle was an ancient one, as important during the Middle Horizon as it was in later Inca times, and as deeply respected by the rulers of the Huari Empire.[4] It is impossible

[4] Menzel, "Style and Time," pp. 70-71.

to say, though, whether the central coast lay outside the boundaries of the empire or whether it was simply a province with an unusually high degree of autonomy.

Pachacamac was not the only settlement that developed into a major city at this time. Other important centers of this time were Cajamarquilla and Vista Alegre in the middle Rimac Valley. These two cities, which faced each other across the Rimac River, were the principal settlements respectively of the northern and southern sides of the valley. The rise of cities on the central coast at this time seems to have signaled the decline of the old ceremonial centers. Beginning in the Middle Horizon, it became a common practice to bury the dead in the old pyramids, digging holes through the adobe surfaces for this purpose. Such a profanation would be unimaginable if the ceremonial centers had continued to function as the centers of society. They may never have completely lost their sacred character, however, even after they were abandoned by their priests and attendants. They were favorite burial grounds from the Middle Horizon until the time the Spaniards arrived, presumably because they were holy soil and therefore advantageous to the dead in their future life.

With the possible exception of Cerro de Trinidad in the Chancay Valley (see p. 118) the settlements mentioned above were the earliest cities built on the central coast. Pachacamac was the most important of them, but it may not have been the largest. Cajamarquilla was a very large settlement which could have housed up to ten thousand persons. But where Pachacamac was occupied continuously until the arrival of the Spaniards, Cajamarquilla and Vista Alegre were abandoned by the end of Epoch 2, about the same time that the city of Huari fell. Their growth into cities corresponded with the arrival of Huari influences on the central coast, and their abandonment was part of the disintegration of the Huari Empire. It seems safe to say, therefore, that the rise of these cities on the central coast was due to the arrival of the urbanized Huari people. The abandonment of the ceremonial centers and the construction of the cities was too carefully timed to have been a coincidence.

THE MARAÑON VALLEY

The middle Marañon region, especially the area of Cajamarca, also seems to have enjoyed special prestige in the Huari Empire. The story begins during Epoch 1, when the empire had not yet expanded so far north. At least one and perhaps three great fortified cities were built in the Marañon Basin at this time. The one definitely dated site is Marca Huamachuco, near the modern city of Huamachuco. It was located on a flat-topped hill. The main portion of the site, an area measuring some 1000 by 650 yards, was surrounded by a stout double fortification wall. Inside the wall was a citadel, a great plaza, a group of rectangular stone towers, and many large two- and three-story residential structures. Similar residences were also built outside the wall, as were a group of circular stone-walled forts and a number of other structures. Similar walled cities at Kollor near Cajamarca and Kuelape near Chacha-poyas have never been dated, but they are so similar to Marca Huamachuco that they may well have been built at the same time.[5] Since the Marañon Basin had not yet been conquered by Huari in Epoch 1, we cannot attribute the building of these cities to the direct influence of the city-dwelling Huari people. The large size and defensive posture of these cities indicate that the Marañon population was brought together into large defensible settlements, and that the reason for urbanization was primarily military. The defense works could have been a reaction to internecine warfare in the Marañon Basin. However, since the aggressive Huari Empire lay only a short distance to the south, and since its northward ex-pansion was successfully stalled during Epochs 1B and 2A, these fortified cities were probably built for the purpose of keeping out the Huari conquerors.

The main structures at Marca Huamachuco were abandoned during Epoch 2, at which time the site was briefly occupied by people who built a number of small houses but who made no use of the fortifications. At about the same time, the Huari garrison/ storehouse site of Viracochapampa was built nearby. In view of

[5] Henri Reichlen and Paule Reichlen, "Recherches Archéologiques dans le Andes de Cajamarca," *Journal de la Société des Américanistes,* Nouvelle Série, XXXVIII (Paris: Au siège de la Société, Musée de l'Homme, 1949), 143.

the evidence of Huari conquest at this time, it is likely that the invaders destroyed the fortress city of Marca Huamachuco and built Viracochapampa as part of the process of pacifying the local population. The small houses of Epoch 2 at Marca Huamachuco would thus represent the impoverished remnant of the people of that once mighty city.

The middle Marañon region seems to have been a center of considerable importance during Epoch 2B, at least insofar as its pottery art is concerned. Pottery in the local Cajamarca III style was traded in large quantity all over northern Peru and as far south as Huari itself. Although it is dangerous to assume that soldiers and potters had a similar history, it is nevertheless tempting to think that the prestige of Cajamarca III pottery was due not only to its beauty, but also to the respect in which the Marañon people were held after their protracted defense of their homeland.

THE NORTH COAST

There is some evidence that the first cities of the north coast were built during the early part of the Middle Horizon. These cities remain to be studied in detail, but the available evidence does suggest a basic change in settlement patterns. The north-central valleys of Huarmey, Culebras, Casma, Santa, Nepeña, and Virú seem never to have had any cities, though three large urban towns were founded in Casma and Nepeña during the Middle Horizon and flourished throughout the Late Intermediate Period. In contrast, some of the largest cities of ancient Peru were occupied during the Late Intermediate Period in the northern area between the Moche and Motupe Valleys. At least three of these cities were built, or at least begun, during the Middle Horizon: Chanchan (Moche Valley), Pacatnamú (Pacasmayo Valley), and Apurlé (Motupe Valley). There is no way of knowing at present how quickly these sites grew into the great cities of Late Intermediate times. Since they represented an entirely new kind of organization on the north coast, and since their construction began at about the time that the region was occupied by the city-dwelling people of Huari, it is a fair guess that they, like the cities of the central coast, represented Huari influence and possibly even the work of Huari architects.

THE FALL OF EMPIRE

At the end of Epoch 2 the city of Huari was abandoned and the Huari Empire broke up. The fall of Huari was reflected in the provinces by the abandonment of such centers as Cajamarquilla and Vista Alegre. During Epochs 3 and 4 there was a resurgence of the old pattern of regional cultures. The long-range communications established during the Huari Empire did not disappear entirely. Thus for example, stylistic ideas that evolved on the central coast during Epochs 3 and 4 spread to the south coast and vice versa. There was, however, no single widespread style equivalent to Viñaque, nor any major center like Huari. The Huari Empire had lived out its brief life span and was gone forever.

It is not possible to say at this time why the Empire was so short lived. The fact that the Tiahuanaco Empire also had a short life suggests that the explanation may lie in some broad factor affecting the whole of the Andes and not just in local conditions in the area of Huari. We do not know whether we should attribute the fall to guerilla warfare in the provinces, to peasant revolt, to barbarians on the margins, to destructive competition between the empires, or to some other cause. In the most general sense we may venture that the early demise of the Middle Horizon empires was due to their lack of experience in organizing an area of such ecological diversity which was broken up by so many formidable natural barriers. This is scarcely an explanation, but no more meaningful statement can be made until a great deal more research has been done in the field.

Whatever the cause of the fall, its impact was dramatic and long lasting. All of the cities of the southern highlands were abandoned, and the population scattered into the countryside. From the end of Epoch 2, about A.D. 800, no more cities existed in southern Peru until the rebuilding of Cuzco late in the fifteenth century. During the intervening period of nearly 700 years, the entire population seems to have lived in villages and small rural towns. Just as the empires were built by the cities, so the reaction against the empires swept away urban life throughout southern Peru.

X

The Interregnum

The Late Intermediate Period (ca. A.D. 1000-1476) was a time of high technological competence and extensive interregional commerce. It was also, for most of Peru, an interregnum between the Huari-Tiahuanaco empires and that of the Incas. The country was again divided into small regional states that were engaged in feuding warfare without, for the most part, consolidating their conquests. The idea of empire was not dead, however. In the latter part of the period the Chimú people of the Moche Valley conquered the coast from Supe northward nearly to the Ecuadorean border and held it until it was wrested from them by the Incas. Though the cities of the south were abandoned, the north and central coast and the Marañon Basin were urbanized.

As usual, cultural relationships are most easily traced through ceramic styles, which show a regionalization as intense as was that of the Early Intermediate Period. Each region—in some cases, each individual coastal valley—had its own distinctive style. Many of the regional styles evolved more or less directly out of the Tiahuanacoid polychrome wares, but there were also strong trends toward archaism and toward the more or less abrupt invention of whole new styles without obvious artistic antecedents. Thus, for

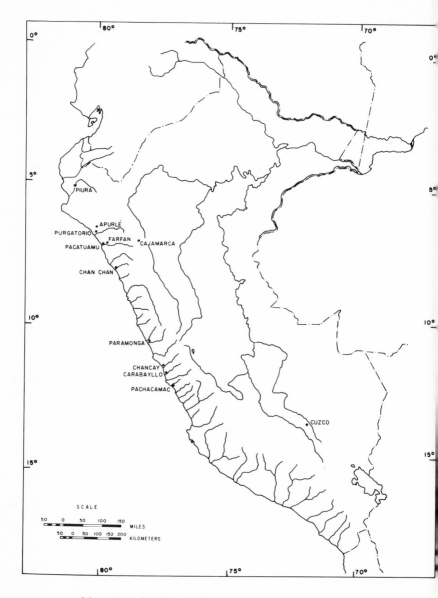

Map 9. Archaeological Sites of the Late Intermediate Period

example, in the Chancay and Huaura Valleys there was a process
first of alteration of the Pachacamac designs and gradually of their
replacement by simplified geometric motifs, together with a progressive discarding of color, culminating in the Chancay black-on-
white style in which the Tiahuanacoid elements had died out by
attrition (Plate 8). On the north-central coast and in the Callejón
de Huaylas, the Huari polychrome designs disappeared abruptly
near the end of the Middle Horizon and were replaced by localized
styles of unpainted brown ware bearing simple plastic ornamentation. A similar process of rejection of the foreign designs, though

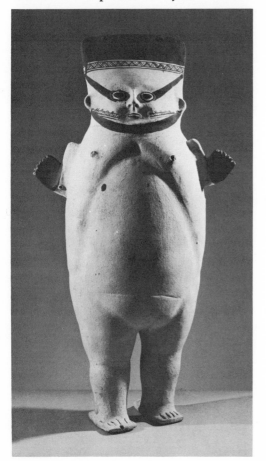

PLATE 8. Large Hollow
Figurine of the Chancay
Black-on-White   Style
(*Courtesy of the Mu-
seum of Primitive Art*)

more gradual, was evident on the north coast, where the Chimu blackware style evolved through progressive revivals of old Moche motifs and vessel forms. The south coastal styles followed a history similar to that of the central coast but—especially in Ica and Nazca —retained the old southern tradition of polychrome painting.

Ceramic technology was now at its best. With a long tradition behind them, the Peruvian potters were intimately acquainted with the plastic and firing properties of their clays, and their wares reflect this knowledge. Throughout most of the country pottery was made by coiling, as it had been since it first was made in the Initial Period. Two special techniques were widely used in the north.

In the paddle-and-anvil method, the vessel was hammered into shape by a wooden or clay paddle, while a cobblestone held inside the growing pot absorbed the blows. This technique was invented on the far north coast during the Early Intermediate Period, and it soon became traditional in that region. Throughout the Middle Horizon, Late Intermediate Period, and Late Horizon, all but the finest vessels were made by paddle-and-anvil technique, and the paddles often bore carved designs stamped on the surface of the pots. Despite the introduction of the potter's wheel by the Spanish, paddle-and-anvil pottery is still made in the Lambayeque and Piura Valleys. The strength of the technological tradition is made clear by the following statement:

> The remarkable thing about this retention of an aboriginal ceramic tradition is that it shows so little influence of the three successive conquests of the region [i.e., Chimu, Inca and Spanish], though the third conquest has drastically revolutionized life in Piura and Chira." [1]

The second northern technique was press molding, in which sections of the vessel were made by pressing plastic clay into partial molds and then joining the sections. This method had been used by the Moche potters of the Early Intermediate Period to reproduce figure-modeled bottles or vessels with low relief designs. Press

[1] Edward P. Lanning, *A Ceramic Sequence for the Piura and Chira Coast, North Peru,* University of California Publications in American Archaeology and Ethnology, XLVI, No. 2 (Berkeley and Los Angeles: University of California Press, 1963), p. 212.

molding was popular in the Middle Horizon from Piura in the far north to Lima on the central coast. It flourished especially in the region of Supe and the Fortaleza Valley, where it was a favorite medium for Tiahuanacoid designs. During most of the Late Intermediate Period it seems to have been largely restricted to the north coast proper—Virú, Moche, Chicama, and Pacasmayo—but the Chimú people again carried it north and south shortly before the Inca conquest, and the Incas themselves may have taken over the technique and spread it still further.

Despite the high level of ceramic technology, artistic standards were generally low. One gets the impression that pottery was now factory-produced in large quantity for purely utilitarian purposes. It was not a medium for great art. There is not one single Late Intermediate Period vessel that can compare with the masterpieces to be found in the Chavín, Nazca, Moche, Viñaque, Pachacamac, and Atarco styles. There were still a few centers where elegant pottery was made and from which it was widely traded as luxury goods. One such "fancy" style was that of Soniche in the Ica Valley; another, apparently, was Cajamarca of the middle Marañon. Even the best of Soniche and Cajamarca ceramic painters, however, were hardly the masters that some of their ancestors had been.

Textile technology had largely evolved during the Early Intermediate Period, but new techniques were added during the Middle Horizon and the Late Intermediate Period. The principal effect of the Middle Horizon empires seems to have been the popularizing of tapestry making all along the coast. Tapestry was the principal medium of the polychrome Tiahuanacoid designs. Although the designs themselves soon disappeared, the tapestry technique remained universally popular during the Late Intermediate Period. It was accompanied by gauze weaving, knotted lace, warp striping, gingham, brocade, embroidery, double and triple cloth, twill, warp patterning, painting, tie-dye, ikat, darning, feather work, and a great many other techniques. The technical quality of the weaving is indicated by the following remarks on tapestry:

> The Peruvian products . . . were technically far superior in every detail [to European tapestries]. . . . they frequently have

PLATE 9. Polychrome Shirt, Ica Valley (*Courtesy of the Museum of Primitive Art*)

over two hundred weft per inch and some exceed two hundred and fifty. . . . It would be impossible to create such a fabric without having perfect yarn for the warp. . . . Roughly, contemporary European tapestry, by contrast, seldom exceeds eighty-five weft per inch, and modern examples much fewer.

. . . The extreme fineness of weave, however, is only one aspect of the Peruvian product. Every conceivable device applicable to tapestry construction was employed with care and skill.[2]

Weaving was obviously a skill of high prestige, as it had been at the Paracas Necropolis and in the Middle Horizon and as it was to be under the Incas. Artistic standards remained high, as witnessed by the predominance of Late Intermediate Period pieces in museum exhibits of ancient Peruvian textiles. Although each region had its own style, as it did in pottery, the differences from region to region were less marked and many motifs were spread over very large areas. It is likely, too, that cloth was more widely traded than was pottery, though no studies of this subject have been made (Plates 9-11).

Metallurgy also reached a peak during the Late Intermediate Period. As we have seen, copper and gold were worked during the

[2] Junius B. Bird, "Techniques," in Bennett and Bird, *Andean Culture History*, p. 277.

PLATE 10. Lace with Bird Designs, Chancay Valley (*Courtesy of the Museum of Primitive Art*)

Early Horizon by a number of techniques. Moche metallurgy, the most sophisticated of the Early Intermediate Period, added silver and various alloys, gilding, open-mold casting, the "lost wax" technique, and copper smelting, as well as the use of copper for such tools as chisels and digging stick points. Silver plating first appeared on the north coast during the Middle Horizon together with a copper-arsenic alloy with bronzelike qualities. True bronze, the alloy of copper and tin, also made its appearance at this time, not in Peru but in northern Argentina. It is generally thought that bronze was of Bolivian origin because most of the tin deposits of the Andes are in Bolivia, and that the early Argentine bronze simply reflects an invention first made on the Bolivian *altiplano*. Copper was used extensively at Tiahuanaco, but so far none of it has proved to have a tin content, so the question of the origins of Andean bronze must remain an open one for the time being.

PLATE 11. Weaver's Work Basket Containing Spindles and Yarn, Chancay Valley (*Courtesy of the Museum of Primitive Art*)

Regardless of its origin, bronze spread widely across Peru during the Late Intermediate Period, though it was still not used to the same extent as copper. In general, the various pure metals and alloys and the various techniques appeared in much the same form throughout Peru in the Late Intermediate Period, though there were still regional preferences, such as the emphasis on gold in the north and on silver on the south coast. Most of the metal work was still ornamental, but such tools as copper and bronze club heads, knives, and digging stick points were made in various parts of Peru.

Architecture was impoverished during the Late Intermediate Period, and it was not to rise again as a great art until the time of the Incas. Statues, stelae, and other architectural ornaments of carved stone, which had begun at Sechín in the Initial Period, seem never again to have been made after the fall of Huari and Tiahuanaco. Dressed stone masonry, so characteristic of the monumental architecture of the Early Horizon, Early Intermediate Period, and Middle Horizon in the highlands, is unknown from the Late Intermediate Period—though the reason for its absence may be a lack of excavation in sites of this period. The great adobe pyramids of the Early Intermediate Period were no longer being built on the coast, though some smaller platform mounds continued to be built. Construction on the coast was now almost entirely of large adobes or packed clay; in the highlands, of field stones. Wattle-and-daub houses were undoubtedly universal, but are little represented in the archaeology, again mainly because of the lack of excavations in habitation sites of the period. Architectural ornament is known only from the coast, and consists exclusively of carved and/or painted murals on clay plaster.

In the field of economics, there was little difference between the Late Intermediate cultures and those of the latter part of the Early Intermediate Period. The basic Andean pattern was fully evolved by A.D. 500 and simply continued unchanged. Hunting was by now probably only a sport of the nobility, as it was later under the Incas. Intensive agriculture and animal husbandry were fully developed, and all of the plants and animals later found by the Spaniards were undoubtedly now being raised. Potatoes, *quinoa, oca,* and *ulluco* were the staples at high altitudes, maize and various root crops at middle altitudes, maize, squash, and beans on the coast. The coastal cotton crop and the highlands alpaca herds provided raw materials for textiles, and llamas and guinea pigs were raised at all altitudes. Fish and shellfish, gathered and processed by specialized villages, continued to be fundamental in the coastal diet. Every coastal valley had its over-all irrigation system, and, on the north coast, some systems manipulated the water of two or more rivers. Though the agricultural terraces of the highlands are largely undated, their construction had surely begun by this time.

Interregional commerce was rather more extensive than it had been during the Early Intermediate Period but less than in the Middle Horizon. The southern obsidian trade was now limited to the highlands, but pottery and fancy textiles were traded over considerable distances. The Soniche pottery style of Ica seems to have been particularly favored by the upper classes, and specimens of it have been found as far north as the Chancay Valley. Some of the ancient roads, usually considered to be part of the Inca "highway" system, were probably built by the Late Intermediate states to facilitate commerce within their borders.

As in other periods, there is no way of estimating population except by general impression. The ancient population had certainly reached its maximum at this time. Every archaeologist who has worked fairly widely in Peru has had the experience of finding Late Intermediate sites wherever he looks, whereas sites of other periods often take more effort to locate. There were a few valleys where the population seems to have declined, but they are rare exceptions to the general rule. In Virú, for example, the population appears to have shrunk to about half of its Early Intermediate size and to have been concentrated on the lower part of the delta.[3] More typical were the valleys of the north-central coast. Though nearly depopulated in the latter part of the Early Intermediate Period, they filled up rapidly during the Middle Horizon and reached their population maximum during the Late Intermediate. Perhaps such exceptional valleys as Virú suffered particularly heavy losses of men of breeding age in the wars of conquest that led to the establishment of the Huari and Chimú empires.

The most profound change in the Late Intermediate Period was in the distribution of urban life. As we have seen, the great cities of the Early Intermediate Period were all in southern Peru. Urbanism was never firmly established on the south coast and did not last into the Middle Horizon in that area. In the southern highlands, on the other hand, the cities were the nucleus of the Tiahuanaco and Huari empires. They were abandoned when the empires fell, and thereafter all of southern Peru was a vast area of purely rural life.

[3] Willey, *Prehistoric Settlement Patterns*, pp. 394-95.

Urban life seems not to have appeared in northern Peru until the Middle Horizon. There is every reason to believe that it grew up in the north as a function of the Huari conquest, either as a defensive reaction, as a copy of the way of life in the capital, or in cities founded by the Huari conquerors. Marca Huamachuco, Kollor, and Kuelape, all in the Marañon drainage, were fortified cities which concentrated a formerly scattered rural population. At least Marca Huamachuco was built during Middle Horizon Epoch 1 and may have been partly responsible for the delay in the northward expansion of the Huari empire. On the central coast, Pachacamac, Cajamarquilla, and Vista Alegre all seem to have grown into cities during the Middle Horizon, but only Pachacamac survived the fall of Huari. No cities were ever built on the north-central coast as far north as Virú. On the north coast, at least Chanchan, Pacatnamú, and Apurlé were founded during the Middle Horizon.

Cities flourished throughout the northern half of Peru in Late Intermediate times. Pachacamac, Kollor, and Kuelape were still occupied. New cities grew up in the Chillón Valley and in the vicinity of Huánuco and Huancayo. It was on the north coast, however, that Late Intermediate urbanism reached its peak. The names of the north coastal cities—Chanchan, Pacatnamú, Farfán, Purgatorio, Apurlé—are practically a roster of the better-known cities of ancient Peru. No wonder that Wendell C. Bennett, whose system of developmental stages was based on the north coastal sequence, used the name "City Builders" for the cultures of this period.[4] Of the north coastal cities, only Chanchan has been extensively excavated; it will be described below.

POLITICS IN THE LATE INTERMEDIATE PERIOD

When we reach the latter part of the Late Intermediate Period, just before the Inca conquest of Peru, we begin to get scraps of historical evidence that are independent of the archaeological record. Some of the Spanish conquerors interviewed Inca historians and people in the provinces, and recorded a few comments on the

[4] Bennett and Bird, *Andean Culture History,* pp. 201-14.

country that the Inca armies found when they built their empire. Not all of the early Spanish chroniclers can be relied on, but the archaeological evidence can be used to verify their reports.

One chronicler who has been particularly influential with archaeologists seems to be unreliable on the subject of pre-Inca states in Peru. He was Garcilaso de la Vega, a half-breed who was born after the conquest and wrote his account in Spain during his old age. Garcilaso told of four coastal "empires": Chimú in the north; Cuismancu in the Chancay, Chillón, and Rimac Valleys of the central coast; Chuquismancu in the Mala, Chilca, and Cañete Valleys of the south-central coast; and Chincha in the Chincha, Pisco, Ica, and Nazca Valleys of the south coast.[5] The existence of these empires has been uncritically accepted by archaeologist after archaeologist.[6] The Chimú Empire is well documented in other early Spanish chronicles and in the archaeological record. Too little late archaeology has been done on the south-central coast to permit a judgment about the Chuquismancu "empire." But archaeological evidence shows that Cuismancu, as defined by Garcilaso, cannot have existed, and it throws serious doubts on the existence of a Chincha "empire." The Chancay culture, characterized by black-on-white pottery and distinctive textiles, was spread through the Huaura and Chancay Valleys, Ancón, and the northern part of the Chillón delta. The "Huancho" culture of the southern Chillón, Rimac, and Lurín Valleys is best known for its crude white-painted and appliqué designs on pottery. The Chancay and "Huancho" areas may each have been politically integrated, but the boundary between them falls exactly in the middle of the supposed Cuismancu "empire." Similarly, each of the four south coastal valleys which Garcilaso placed in the Chincha "empire" had its own distinctive ceramic style, and the distribution of the styles suggests restricted trade of luxury objects rather than political unification.

Those chroniclers who dealt with the pre-Inca organization of Peru all confirmed the existence of a Chimú empire in the north, but they did not agree as to its exact boundaries. To the north it

[5] Garcilaso de la Vega, Los Comentarios Reales de los Incas, II (Lima: Librería e Imprenta Gil, S. A., 1942), 204, 208.

[6] Bennett and Bird, Andean Culture History, pp. 203-4; Mason, Ancient Civilizations, pp. 100-2; Bushnell, Peru, p. 110.

extended to Tumbes, but the southern limit is variously given in the Huarmey, Fortaleza, or Chillón Valleys. Archaeological evidence of the distribution of Chimú pottery in pure lots—as distinct from occasional trade pieces—suggests a maximum extent from the Chira Valley in the far north to Supe on the north-central coast. The "fortress" of Paramonga (actually probably a temple) is often cited as a border outpost, but the southern boundary seems to have lain somewhat further south. If the Chimú people ever conquered part of the central coast, they cannot have held it for more than a few years before the arrival of the Incas, because they left no evidence of their presence there—not even at the supposed border city of Carabayllo in the northern Chillón Valley.

The first Chimú emperor, Ñançen-pinco, conquered the coast from Saña to Santa. John H. Rowe has estimated a date of A.D. 1370 for this first expansion, which leaves about a century for the accumulation of the abundant Chimú archaeological remains in the area.[7] The last emperor, Minchançaman, embarked on a new program of conquest that was soon to be cut short by the arrival of the Incas.

Chanchan, the capital of the Chimú empire, was the largest city ever built in ancient Peru. It was located on the lower delta of the Moche River near the modern city of Trujillo. The site covers an area of at least six square miles, part of which was apparently occupied during the early stages of its growth and all of which was inhabited when the empire reached its greatest extent. Chanchan was laid out in ten or more large walled compounds containing streets, houses, reservoirs, platform mounds, and other public structures. These compounds averaged about twenty acres in area, and the largest of them covered an area of some forty-five acres. Cemeteries, garden plots, and smaller residential units were distributed within and between the compounds.

Besides Chanchan, four smaller Chimú cities and a number of large dispersed communities and garrison quarters have been reported in the area between the Moche and Motupe Valleys. The cities are Pacatnamú and Farfán in the Pacasmayo Valley, Purgatorio in the Leche Valley, and Apurlé in the Motupe Valley. All

[7] John H. Rowe, "The Kingdom of Chimor," *Acta Americana*, VI, Nos. 1-2 (1948), 40.

of them show the same formal planning and large walled compounds as at Chanchan. Occasional walled compounds, presumably representing residences of the nobility, were interspersed in some of the dispersed communities.

Archaeologists have been puzzled by the contrast between the great cities of the north coast and the rural organization of the south coast during the Late Intermediate Period. Attempts to minimize the differences usually involve using the term "urban" in reference to such sites as La Centinela in the Chincha Valley and Tambo Colorado in the Pisco Valley,[8] but neither of these settlements was remotely near being a city, and at least Tambo Colorado belongs to the Late Horizon and may have been built by the Incas (Plate 12). Or, the difference has been explained as due

PLATE 12. Patio at Tambo Colorado, Pisco Valley

to the greater amount of water in the northern rivers.[9] However, with the exception of the Tumbes and Chira rivers in the far north and the Santa, which runs through the Callejón de Huaylas, there was no great difference in the water available in the north and south—and the three exceptional rivers lay outside the area of

[8] Bennett and Bird, *Andean Culture History*, p. 206.
[9] Mason, *Ancient Civilizations*, p. 102.

Late Intermediate urbanization. A comparison of three large urbanized northern valleys (Moche, Pacasmayo, and Lambayeque) with three large rural southern valleys (Cañete, Pisco, and Ica) shows a combined average annual run-off of 2321 million cubic meters for the north, 3374 million cubic meters for the south. The irrigated land in the same valleys covers an area of 55,000 hectares in the north, 44,000 in the south.[10] The Late Intermediate population was also probably about the same for each area. As we have seen, though, it was distributed in entirely different living patterns.

Since there was no significant ecological difference between north and south, the difference in settlement patterns is best seen as a function of the culture history of each area. The south coast, which had shared in the development of southern cities during the Early Intermediate Period, was closely linked to Huari in spite of its lack of Middle Horizon cities. When the empire fell, the south coastal valleys were caught up in the process of ruralization which swept southern Peru as a whole. During the Late Intermediate Period, the Ica Valley developed a pattern of ceremonial centers and dispersed communities very similar to that which had dominated the north in the Early Intermediate Period. In contrast, the north coast seems to have been only loosely linked into the Huari Empire. Whether or not its cities were founded by the Huari conquerors, the dissolution of the empire left them not only inhabited but free to pursue the course of imperialism (and attendant urban growth) which they had taken over from the southern invaders.

In the highlands the attention of archaeologists has always been directed primarily toward the earlier and more spectacular urban cultures. The Spanish chroniclers, however, recorded the official Inca version of southern highlands political relations just before the Inca expansion. Behind a façade of self-glorification and manifest destiny, we get a picture of numerous small tribal groups engaged in constant feuds, shifting their alliances as the occasion dictated. This picture agrees well with that of the archaeological record, where we see a heterogeneous rural society that cannot yet

---

[10] Alfred L. Kroeber, *Archaeological Explorations in Peru, Part II, The Northern Coast,* Anthropology Memoirs, II, No. 2 (Chicago: Field Museum of Natural History, 1930), p. 76.

have entirely forgotten the glories of the days of empire. In such a situation, it was perhaps inevitable that some one tribal group would eventually embark on the conquest of a new empire. As chance and history would have it, this group was the Incas.

XI

The Incas

The Incas were one of several small tribal states in the southern highlands which were engaged in a power struggle in the early part of the fifteen century A.D. The principal peoples competing with them were the Chanca and Quechua in the Apurimac Basin to the west, and the Lupaca and Colla in the Titicaca Basin to the south. The Incas got their start by defeating the Chancas when the latter attacked Cuzco about 1438. Pachacuti Inca Yupanqui, who commanded the Inca troops in the defense of Cuzco, was crowned king and immediately undertook the expansion of Inca territory through conquest.

The fascinating story of the Inca conquest of Peru, as told by the Inca historians to their Spanish conquerors, can only be summarized here.[1] After the defeat of the Chancas, the Incas emerged as the strongest military power in the southern highlands and the only one with an interest in retaining and organizing conquered territory rather than just looting it and withdrawing. During the twenty-five years following the defense of Cuzco, the Inca armies under Pachacuti conquered the western Titicaca Basin and almost all of the Urubamba, Apurimac, and Mantaro Basins. The con-

[1] For a fuller version, see Rowe, "Inca Culture," pp. 201-9.

quest of the Colla was entrusted to the Chancas,· who also participated in the Mantaro campaign. General Capac Yupanqui, who led the army into the Mantaro, also invaded Cajamarca (a highlands state allied to the Chimú empire), took the city, and left a garrison there. This battle, in which a contingent of Chimú troops helped defend Cajamarca, marked the first face-to-face meeting of the expanding empires of Cuzco and Chanchan.

With the core of the south highlands under control and the new provinces contributing manpower and logistical support, the Inca army became a steamroller which perhaps could only have been stopped by the army of Chimú if circumstances had permitted an early encounter between the two. While Cuzco was engulfing the south highlands, however, Chanchan was engrossed in the conquest and consolidation of the northern half of the coast. By the time the two met the Incas had grown so strong that the outcome was inevitable.

Early in the 1460's Pachacuti's son Topa Inca took charge of the army, while Pachacuti concentrated on rebuilding Cuzco and organizing an administrative system for the new empire. In his first campaign, Topa Inca marched northward to relieve the Cajamarca garrison, conquering the highlands as far north as Quito in modern Ecuador. Moving down to the coast, the Incas invaded Chimú from the north and marched in triumph through the whole length of the Chimu kingdom and south to the Lurín Valley, taking Minchançaman to Cuzco as a prisoner.

Topa Inca, who succeeded to the throne in 1471, extended the empire nearly to its ultimate limits (Map 10). In successive campaigns he took the south coast of Peru; smashed a major uprising in the Titicaca Basin; conquered the whole of highlands Bolivia, northwestern Argentina, and northern Chile south to the Maule River; and twice invaded the *montaña*, though the Incas never incorporated any great area of the tropical forest into their empire. Topa Inca also carried on his father's work of organizing the new territory.

When Topa Inca died about 1483 the crown went to his son Huayna Capac. The latter conquered relatively small areas around Chachapoyas, on the southern coast of Ecuador, and in northern Ecuador up to the Ancasmayo River, rounding out the empire to

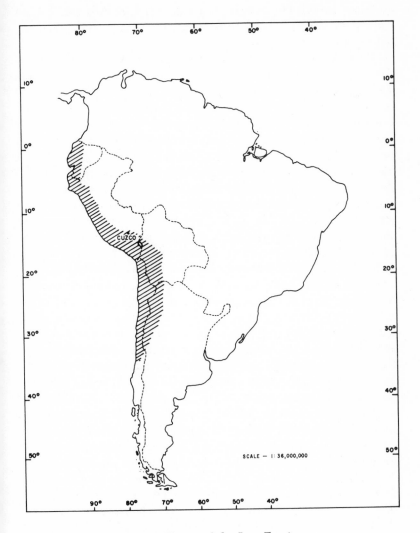

MAP 10. Extent of the Inca Empire

its fullest extent. He also faced and defeated the first attack from outside the borders, that by the "wild" Chiriguano Indians in the southeast.

We have an enormous amount of historical information about the Incas, enough to fill volumes far larger than the present one. Though the Incas were unacquainted with writing, they did not lack historians. The job of historian was a hereditary one, and consisted of memorizing masses of information and repeating it at the request of government officials. Fortunately the early Spanish priests and conquerors recorded many of their observations of Inca life and interviewed numerous Indians, writing down the results almost verbatim. The history of the Inca conquest, so briefly summarized above, has come down to us chiefly as a result of Spanish interviews of the Inca historians. In addition, there were innumerable early chroniclers who left a record of life in the Inca Empire. Most of them describe life in the capital, but a few report on the provinces. Not all of the early Spanish chroniclers were good observers or reliable reporters, and they tended to borrow information from each other without following the modern practice of citing their sources. Careful comparison of their writings, however, shows who was borrowing from whom, who was overexcercising his imagination, and which information was repeated independently and therefore was probably accurate. Happily, a number of such comparative studies have been made, and we can talk with confidence about many aspects of Inca life.[2] The paragraphs that follow do not pretend to cover the whole subject, but rather concentrate on those themes which, because they can be inferred from the archaeological record, have been the subject of our discussion of earlier periods.

The population of the Inca Empire, including its Ecuadorian, Bolivian, Argentine, and Chilean provinces, has been estimated at 6,000,000 persons. The Rimac Valley had a population of 150,000; the Chincha Valley 50,000; the Virú Valley 25,000.[3] Peru proper must have had close to 5 million of the total, of whom perhaps half lived on the coast.

[2] Rowe, "Inca Culture"; Mason, *Ancient Civilizations,* Chaps. VII-XIV.
[3] Rowe, "Inca Culture," pp. 184-85; Willey, *Prehistoric Settlement Patterns,* p. 395.

Agriculture and animal husbandry were highly organized under the Incas. The coastal irrigation systems, though largely built in earlier periods, were now run by a single central authority. Irrigation and hillside terraces also extended the range of highland farm land, though not so dramatically as on the coast. Agricultural terraces were particularly important in small, narrow valleys, whereas in the larger basins they added only a relatively small amount to the total farm land. Terraces surely did not account for as much as 25 per cent of the total agricultural acreage in the highlands. The rest was bottom land primarily in the larger valleys. John V. Murra has shown that, in the highlands, terracing, irrigation, and fertilizer were all associated primarily with the cultivation of maize, which had a special status and ritual significance to the Incas.[4] Classic Inca terraces were carefully faced with stone and had stone-lined channels to bring the irrigation water. Highlands rivers were also canalized with stone walls and sometimes with stone paving.

An important Inca invention was the *taclla* or "foot plow," a long pole with a bronze point, a foot rest, and a handle. Though the *taclla* was essentially only a large, glorified digging stick, it permitted the soil to be turned as with a plow rather than simply perforated for the planting of seeds. A line of men worked across the field, driving the *tacllas* in, turning up the soil, stepping back a pace, and repeating the process, while a line of women faced them breaking up the clods with clubs or hoes. On a small plot, a single man and woman might perform this operation. The same techniques are still widely used by Andean Indians today.

The Incas divided farm land into three parts—for the state, the church, and the farmers. The public fields were worked first, after which the farmer was free to plant or harvest his own crops. The produce of the public lands was stored in government storehouses where it served to feed the army, the government with its countless specialists, and the priests and their attendants. In addition, the storehouses provided a surplus which was distributed to any region suffering a shortage of food. Though life was strictly regimented, no one starved under the Incas.

[4] John V. Murra, "Rite and Crop in the Inca State," in *Culture in History, Essays in Honor of Paul Radin*, ed. Stanley Diamond (New York: Columbia University Press, 1960), pp. 393-407.

As in earlier periods, llamas, alpacas, guinea pigs, muscovy ducks, and dogs were raised in large quantities to provide meat, wool, transport, and animals for sacrifices. The guinea pig was probably the major source of meat. Llamas and alpacas were pastured on the high *puna* as they are today. Archaeological evidence also shows that, during the Late Intermediate Period and in the Late Horizon, herds of llamas were kept during the winter in the remaining areas of *lomas* vegetation on the coast—a pasturing arrangement which is still used for goats.

Hunting was now reserved as a sport for the nobility. The emperor kept game preserves that were occasionally thrown open for communal hunts by the nobles. Hunting was done with slings, bolas, snares, nooses, clubs, and nets for birds. On the coast, fishing and shellfishing continued to provide a major part of the diet, and the specialized fishing villages were among the few settlements whose way of life seems to have been largely unaffected by the Inca conquest.

Inca techniques of food preparation have all come down to the present day in the Andean highlands. Food was either roasted or else boiled in the form of soups or stews. Potatoes were preserved by alternately freezing and drying them, which produced a shriveled floury product called *chuño*. The Incas also invented jerked meat, which they called *charqui*. Maize, *quinoa, oca,* and *molle* were made into beer or *chicha*. Grains were ground with a rocker mill, a device that had first appeared in the Early Intermediate Period. It consisted of a large flat nether stone and a crescentic upper stone that was rocked back and forth on its curved side. Unlike the rotary mill of the Old World, the rocker mill was not adaptable to mechanization, but it was the most efficient hand-run grinder ever invented, producing flour with a minimum of effort.

The Incas came from the rural tradition of the south. When Pachacuti and Topa Inca rebuilt Cuzco, they created it in the rural image. Its center was essentially a ceremonial center, containing temples, palaces and government buildings but no residences for anyone but royalty, priests, and their immediate retainers. The rest of the population was distributed in villages spaced more or less evenly around the center and separated from it by farm lands or garden plots. The villages were drawn in closely enough, however, and were so integral a part of the plan of Cuzco that one might be justified in calling the whole a semiagglutinated city rather than a ceremonial center with attendant villages. If so, it was the only city in ancient Peru that ever grew up in this fashion. It was also the only city ever built or occupied in the southern half of Peru between the fall of Huari and the arrival of the Spanish.

It is doubtful if the Incas ever built any settlement larger than a small town. Spectacular as Inca sites may have been in their dressed stone masonry, those outside of Cuzco all tend to be quite small. In cases where a provincial population was scattered, the Inca rulers tried to concentrate it in larger settlements. Even these relocation sites, however, probably seldom exceeded a population of 1000 persons. Only when the Incas built administrative centers in already-existing cities could they be considered an urban people.

Most of the older cities were abandoned during the Late Horizon, either destroyed during the wars of conquest or depopulated because of the Incas' policy of settling their subjects in villages (neither archaeology nor the chroniclers tell us which). City life was not entirely dead in Peru, as there were substantial urban settlements at Carabayllo in the Chillón Valley, near Huancayo in the Mantaro Basin, and at Huánuco in the Huallaga Basin. On the whole, however, urbanism reached a low point during the Late Horizon. Intensive as the Inca organization may have been, it stressed the rural mode of life. The distribution of the population in villages and small towns is reminiscent of medieval Europe, though it was based on an entirely different social and political organization.

We do not know whether the great north coastal cities were entirely abandoned, or whether they retained a fraction of their population after the Inca conquest. The Inca administrative centers, garrison quarters, and storehouses in this region were not built in the cities, but out in the countryside or within dispersed communities. The Inca sites were usually located in defensible positions on steep hill slopes, which suggests that the Incas may have had doubts about the loyalty of their Chimú subjects.

The typical Inca residential unit was a rectangular walled compound containing several houses. Such compounds had long been made on the north coast, and the Incas may have adopted them after their conquest of the Chimú Empire. Houses were made of stones or adobes, with steep thatched roofs. Field stones were used in commoners' houses, dressed stones in those of the nobility.

Public constructions included such buildings as palaces, temples, granaries, fortresses, barracks for the army, and wayside stations on the highways. The finest efforts of the stone mason's art were lavished on these structures. Stone blocks, sometimes of gigantic size, were individually cut and beveled to fit tightly without the use of mortar (Plate 13). The blocks were trimmed with stone

PLATE 13. Mortarless Stone Construction at Inca Fortress of Sacsahuaman, Cuzco

hammers, hauled on wooden rollers, and raised into place on earth ramps. The Incas knew and used the plumb bob, and made bronze crowbars and chisels for use in construction activities.

The local nobility of some of the coastal valleys built large residential compounds in imitation of Inca palaces. These manor houses were located in the valley bottoms, where—in contrast to the dispersed communities of the peasantry—they usurped land that would have been useful for farming. This deliberate waste of arable land can only be seen as a symbolic reinforcement of the social position of the owners. The manor houses of the Late Horizon set a precedent which was soon to be taken up by the Spanish conquerors and which has survived today in the *hacienda* houses of the affluent landowners.

Except for mortarless masonry, the plumb bob, and the *taclla,* the Incas made no technological inventions. Even the beam balance, one of the most typical of Inca artifacts, is known from the Middle Horizon at Ancón. The Incas contributed to technology not as inventors but as organizers. Useful tools and techniques were now spread from one end of the empire to the other. Perhaps the Incas' most important contribution was in the field of metallurgy. In earlier periods, metal had been used primarily for ornaments, seldom for tools. The favorite metals had been gold, silver, copper, and alloys of the three. Bronze—the hardest metal known in ancient Peru—was not at all common. The Incas popularized the use of bronze for crowbars, chisels, axes, club heads, *taclla* points, and knives (Plate 14). Under their reign stone tools began to lose importance and bronze tools became available to the ordinary farmer.

The Incas, faced with the task of governing their vast new ter-

PLATE 14. Inca Bronze Knife (*Courtesy of the Museum of Primitive Art*)

ritory, borrowed some organizational principles from Chimú and invented a great many more. Acting on the basis of an old Andean tradition, they founded a new system of hereditary social classes and put the government in the hands of its higher echelons. The emperor himself was the final authority in every matter, both public and private. Below him there was an upper nobility, called *Inca* or *Pakoyoc,* including the descendants of former emperors and many "Incas by privilege." A lower nobility, the *Curacas,* consisted of local and regional administrative officials and included natives of the provinces. The class of commoners consisted of the great mass of farmers, herders, and fishermen who made up the population of the empire. Luxury craftsmen, accountants, historians, and other government servants comprised a special hereditary class, exempt from taxation and supported by the government. Since the Incas used no money, the commoners payed taxes in labor, working the fields of the government and the church, building and maintaining roads and bridges, serving in the army, and so forth.

The early Spanish chronicles comment repeatedly on the organization and efficiency of the Inca government. The entire population of the empire was rigorously organized in a decimal system, with administrative officers for every unit of taxpayers from 10 to 10,000. The government kept a careful, up-to-date census of population, farm land, and domestic animals, and administrative decisions were made on the basis of detailed knowledge of the people being governed. The Incas, like their predecessors, were unacquainted with writing. Indeed, the efficiency of the Inca government may well have been due to the fact that its records were verbal, thus eliminating quintuplicate forms and multiple signatures.

One key to successful government was the *quipu,* a set of knotted strings used for recording numbers. The *quipu* consisted of a main cord from which hung several secondary strings. Numbers were recorded by tying knots in the pendent strings, the position of the knots indicating their place in the decimal system, the number of knots showing the number of units at that place. Zero was indicated by leaving a position empty, without knots. Thus, for example, the number 4039 would be represented by four knots in the thousands place, none in the hundreds place, three in the tens place, and nine in the digits place. A special hereditary class of accountants memorized the meaning of the numbers and interpreted them when required by government officials. Messengers carried *quipus* as aids to memory, and the government historians also used them to record statistics in their memorized histories.

The Incas pursued a course designed to break up old tribal loyalties and to integrate the whole population of the empire into a new national state. While imposing their own religion, they adopted local gods into their pantheon. They often maintained local rulers as puppet governors, but took their sons to Cuzco to educate them as Incas and thus guarantee a loyal government in the future. Whenever they conquered a new province, they sent in colonies of loyal subjects and moved the more obstreperous native elements to distant parts of the empire. This process of colonization was carried on on such a vast scale that, when the Spaniards arrived, the old tribal groups and languages were fast disappearing. In a span of less than seventy-five years the Incas greatly changed the ethnic and cultural makeup of their whole empire.

Trade in foodstuffs and other essentials was purely local. Luxury goods, on the other hand, were carried from one end of the empire to the other. In theory they all belonged to the emperor, and in practice they were reserved for the nobility. In order to facilitate communications and the flow of luxury goods, the Incas linked up the empire with a system of roads aimed to speed up foot travel. There were two main north-south highways, one on the coast and one in the highlands, and every town and village was linked into the highways by a network of lesser roads. Where the highways crossed hills they were cut out of bedrock and often protected by retaining walls. In low places they were built up on causeways that were perforated by stone-lined culverts. The highways were sometimes paved with flat stones. On particularly steep hills stone steps were built or the highway was cut in a zigzag. Government messages were relayed by runners stationed about a kilometer apart, each runner memorizing the message and running it on to the next post. Road houses (*tambos*) were built along the highway at distances of a day's journey from each other. Narrow rivers were crossed by log bridges, wide rivers by suspension bridges. The latter were made of cables braided of twigs and vines and hung from stone towers on each side of the river.

Coastwise shipping was limited to the far northern part of the empire. Large balsa wood rafts, propelled by sails and oars and steered by an ingenious system of center boards, were built in the Gulf of Guayaquil. These rafts, capable of carrying very substantial cargoes, traveled northward along the coast as far as Central America. There is no evidence that they ever traded southward, where there was no material for their construction and where they would have had to beat against the current. Some large, elaborately carved wooden artifacts from the south coast have sometimes been interpreted as center boards from balsa rafts. I have had opportunity to examine a number of these specimens at the R. H. Lowie Museum in Berkeley. All of them show the same sort of wear around the bottom edge which is commonly exhibited by ancient agricultural implements from Peru. They must have been ceremonial *tacllas,* used for the annual ritual of breaking ground in the spring (Plate 15).

The Incas made their conquest through a combination of military might and diplomacy. Before sending the army into new territory they often sent emissaries who pointed out the advantages of peaceful submission. Where this failed, the army—the strongest military power in the Andes—moved in. Victory was guaranteed by sheer number of troops and by the effectiveness of their supply system. Inca soldiers wore quilted cotton armor, used slings and bolas as artillery, and fought hand to hand with war clubs and "head breakers" consisting of heavy weights tied to stout thongs. Coastal contingents used the spearthrower, and companies of bowmen were imported from the *montaña.*

Settlements were defended by hilltop fortresses to which the population could retreat in times of emergency—an ancient Andean practice going back to the Early Horizon. The most famous of these fortresses is Sacsahuaman, which was built by Pachacuti and Topa Inca on a hill at the edge of Cuzco. The stone walls at Sacsahuaman were set in zigzag fashion so that the defenders would always have a view of an attacker's back. With the fortresses available for retreat, Inca settlements themselves were not fortified in spite of the importance of this practice in earlier periods.

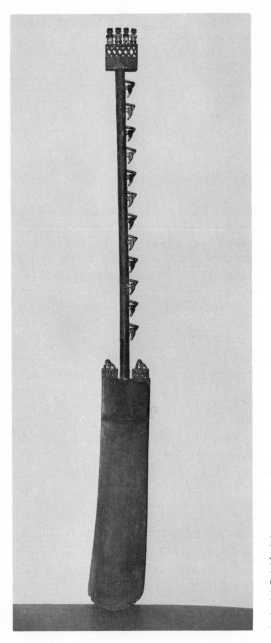

PLATE 15. Ceremonial Agricultural Implement, Painted Wood with Gold and Silver Overlays (*Courtesy of the Museum of Primitive Art*)

The old center of Pachacamac on the central coast, though largely depopulated, continued to enjoy a special position in the empire. The city seems to have shrunk after the Inca conquest to little more than a ceremonial center, but it was a very important ceremonial center. The Incas not only permitted the old oracle to function, but they consulted it themselves and built a new temple at Pachacamac. The archaeological evidence here confirms the statements of the chroniclers. One Spanish soldier reported on Pachacamac as follows:

> . . . though the Inca kings built not only the temple of Cuzco but many others . . . none was equal to that of Pachacama . . . . The priests were very esteemed, and the lords and chiefs obeyed their orders in many matters; and . . . near the temple there were many large quarters for those who came on pilgrimage . . . . When they celebrated the year's great festivals many people came together. . . . the Incas . . . seeing the grandeur of the temple and its great antiquity, and the authority which it had with all the people of the region, and the great devotion which everyone showed to it . . . dealt with the native lords and with the ministers of their god or devil [so] that the temple of Pachacama might keep its authority and service, so long as another temple for the sun be built in the most prominent place; and when the temple of the sun had been built as the Incas ordered, it grew very rich . . . .[5]

Another important center was at Quito in modern Ecuador. Here Huayna Capac established a second capital to facilitate the governing of the far-flung northern provinces. It was at Quito that Huayna Capac died without leaving the succession to the throne clearly defined, and at Quito began the civil war that led to the downfall of the empire.

The distribution of objects in Inca style shows a pattern typical of the imperial styles of ancient Peru. Throughout the provinces, objects—especially pottery vessels—in Inca style were concentrated in the administrative centers, temples, storehouses, garrison quarters, and roadside stations which represented the authority of

[5] Pedro Cieza de León, *La Crónica del Perú* (Buenos Aires and Mexico: Espasa-Calpe Argentina, S.A., 1945), pp. 203-4.

Cuzco. The local nobility tended to live near the Inca centers. The ceramics and textiles at their sites show a mixture of Inca and imitation Inca pieces with new local luxury styles which owed little to the traditional styles of the region. The latter—the old traditional styles—continued to be made in debased form, with at least some degree of Inca influence in their designs, and they were concentrated in the residential areas of the peasantry. The wholehearted adoption of things Inca by the local nobility may be taken as a measure of the success of the Inca administrative system.

THE SPANISH CONQUEST

A small corps of Spaniards under Francisco Pizarro invaded Peru in 1532. In six short years, they conquered the whole of the Inca Empire, looted it of all the gold and silver in sight, and drove the last remnants of the Inca government into exile in the *montaña*. Their feat was one of the most spectacular military accomplishments in the history of man.[6]

How could a handful of adventurous Europeans take over the mightiest empire of ancient America? Though they used both horses and firearms, they were scarcely better armed, armored, or organized than their Inca opponents and they were vastly outnumbered in the bargain. The answer lies, not in European military superiority, but in a concatenation of circumstances which, though they affected the outcome of the conquest, arose independently of it. Four principle factors combined to give the Spanish the victory.

First and most important, Pizarro and his men arrived just at the end of a disastrous civil war. Huayna Capac had died in 1527 without leaving clear the succession to the throne. Two of his sons, Huascar and Atahuallpa, rived the empire through five bloody years. The Spanish arrived just as Atahuallpa's army had won the final decisive battle, but enmities were still strong and either side was willing to make an alliance with the newcomers against the other.

Secondly, the Spaniards found allies among some of the disaffected provincial people. The Cañari of Ecuador, for example,

---

[6] The best telling of the story is still that by William H. Prescott, *History of the Conquest of Peru* (New York: Boston, Phillips, Sampson and Co., 1847).

had suffered Atahuallpa's wrath during the civil war and they eagerly joined the Spanish in their march on Cuzco. In the first years of the conquest, before Spanish reinforcements began to arrive *en masse,* the invading army could well have been described as an Indian army under Spanish command.

In addition the Incas were weakened by a series of epidemics that swept through the empire. They were caused by European diseases, such as smallpox and measles, to which the Indians had no immunity. Starting in Central America, these diseases swept down across South America in great waves, debilitating and demoralizing the Inca defenders. The Inca civil war itself was, in a sense, a result of the epidemics, since Huayna Capac's sudden death was due to the first epidemic, which arrived in Peru before the Spaniards who had originally carried it.

Finally, there was an important difference in diplomatic tactics which worked to the Spaniards' advantage. The Incas had always fought by a traditional code which had served them well, announcing their coming and attempting to frighten their enemies into submission. There was never any doubt about their intentions. The Spanish, militarily weak, looking for gold and not territory as such, chose to hide their intentions in the guise of a diplomatic mission. Any European power would have been suspicious of them, but these tactics were new to the Incas. By the time the conquerors' role became clear, Atahuallpa had been kidnapped and his armies were paralyzed in fear for his safety.

Here ends the story of ancient Peruvian civilization. The Spanish conquest was consolidated by 1538 and the Incas, in spite of resistance in exile and a series of bloody uprisings in the seventeenth and eighteenth centuries, never succeeded in breaking the grip of their conquerors. After 1538, the history of Peru became part of the history of Europe and of modern America.

XII

The Nature of
Peruvian Civilization

Now that we have finished our chronological examination of Peruvian culture history, it is time to look at the record and see if we can make sense out of the welter of archaeological sites, cultures, and sequences.

Because we are civilized, and because civilization has so successfully spread over most of the world, we tend to take it for granted as the "natural" human condition. It is, however, neither more nor less natural than any other way of life. Civilization has grown up, and sometimes disappeared, at particular places and times and for particular reasons. Having come into being, it has spread round the world as it were by contagion. The first civilized men appeared in Mesopotamia only about 5000 years ago—the last ¼ of 1 per cent of man's span on earth—and it is only during the last few centuries that civilization has spread across most of the earth. The speed with which it has replaced other ways of life testifies to its being a marvelous adaptive system.

Something so new is sufficiently "unnatural" that its nature and causes are fit subject for inquiry. This writer will not be so bold as to essay a general theory of civilization. An examination of the growth of civilization in Peru, however, may shed some light on the broad question, "Why civilization?" as well as on the more specific question, "Why civilization in Peru?"

Archaeologists working in the Near East have tended to stress food production (i.e., cultivation and animal husbandry) as the basic cause of civilization.[1] Students of ancient Mexico explain civilization there as a mechanism to control trade between different environmental zones, each of which produced certain crops or goods that the others needed.[2] Another theory holds that irrigation was the motivating force behind the ancient civilizations, that both cities and states grew up as means of controlling the distribution of water.[3] The most comprehensive theory recognizes the importance of both irrigation and commerce between different microenvironments, and also stresses the importance of population size and distribution.[4]

All of these factors have been important in the growth of civilization, but none of them, by itself, is an adequate explanation. All civilizations have been based on food production, but many food-producing peoples never developed civilization, so cultivation and domestication alone are not sufficient causes. In the same way, not all trading systems between different microenvironments have spurred the development of civilization, nor have all irrigation systems done so. Also, systems of trade and water control have sometimes developed after the rise of cities and states, which indicates that they may have been more effects than causes. Population density is an important determinant of sociopolitical structure, but it must be seen in conjunction with other factors.

[1] Robert J. Braidwood and Charles A. Reed, "The Achievement and Early Consequences of Food-Production: A Consideration of the Archeological and Natural-Historical Evidence," *Cold Spring Harbor Symposia on Quantitative Biology*, XXII (1957), 19-31.

[2] Michael D. Coe, "Social Typology and the Tropical Forest Civilizations," *Comparative Studies in Society and History*, IV, No. 1 (1961), 65-85.

[3] Karl A. Wittfogel, "Developmental Aspects of Hydraulic Civilizations," in *Irrigation Civilizations: A Comparative Study*. Social Science Monographs, I (Washington, D.C.: Pan American Union, 1955), 43-52.

[4] William T. Sanders, *The Cultural Ecology of the Teotihuacán Valley* (State College: The Pennsylvania State University, 1965), pp. 192-200.

Civilization has had multiple causes. Its growth has been conditioned by many factors interacting in complex ways, reinforcing or deterring each other. Only some of these factors have been active in any given situation. The tropical forest civilization of the lowland Maya, for example, grew out of a different background and underwent different processes of development than the mountain civilizations of Peru or the alluvial civilizations of Egypt and China. The job of explaining civilization is not a matter of finding some one universal cause. Rather, one must delimit the various kinds of conditions under which civilization has developed and then search out those events which have regularly occurred in each of these situations and those which have occurred in all of them. Equally important, one must attempt to discover which of these events did *not* happen in areas where, under similar circumstances, civilization did not develop.

With these conditions in mind, let us return to the subject of our inquiry and examine some of the factors operative in the development of Peruvian civilization.

THE ENVIRONMENT

The key features of the Peruvian environment were its climatic and topographic extremes, the isolation of the habitable areas, the wealth of natural resources in certain environmental zones, and—during preceramic times—a number of changes including the retreat of the mountain glaciers, the progressive drying out of the whole country, and the lifting of the coastal fog belt.

The climatic changes extended the habitable land in the highlands by making the higher altitudes available for human exploitation, as at Lauricocha. On the coast, on the other hand, these changes led to the gradual disappearance of the fog meadows and the restriction of the population to the seashore and the river valleys. Life in the *lomas* lasted for nearly 5000 years and was not abandoned until the fog meadows had shrunk to the point that they could no longer maintain a human community throughout the winter. The limited resources of the *lomas* had long restricted the size of the coastal population. It was only when man was forced out of the *lomas* and into more productive zones that the brakes were released and the population began the expansion which made civilization inevitable.

Productivity can only be assessed in relation to the food-getting techniques that are in use. For people with hunting and gathering economies, such as those who first inhabited Peru, the resources of the sea and shore were the richest anywhere in Peru. They were not exploited until Preceramic Period V, nor fundamentally important until Period VI. Once the move to the shore was made, the abundant year-round food supply and the absence of natural enemies led to a rapid increase of population until, by the Early Horizon, there were more people on the coast than the shore could support. Without new resources, the population might have leveled off and civilization might never have been achieved; with the valleys waiting to be farmed, the population explosion went on undeterred on a new economic base.

During Periods V and VI and the Initial Period, the coastal valleys provided land for the raising of cotton, gourds, and small amounts of food crops. As the population grew too large to be fed by littoral harvesting, the valleys served as safety valves—places where people moved in search of new food sources. The new sources involved farming and, ultimately, irrigation, and they turned out to be even more productive than littoral harvesting. The Peruvian coastal valleys, given water and a little fertilizer, were among the most fertile land anywhere in the world. Once the techniques were worked out in the Early Horizon and Early Intermediate Period, the continued growth of population—and with it of civilization—was assured.

The highlands valleys were no less fertile than those of the coast, but unfortunately highlands archaeology has not been so well studied. We know that small bands of hunters lived there during Preceramic Periods III-V, and that by the Initial Period the larger highlands basins were occupied by farmers who were progressing toward civilization as rapidly as were the people of the coastal valleys. Unfortunately, we know almost nothing about the transition from hunting to intensive farming in the highlands. All we can say is that, once the change had been made, the production of carbohydrates so far exceeded that of preceramic times as to unleash a population explosion equivalent to that taking place on the coast.

The extremes of altitude and rainfall, characteristic of the Andean environment, also played an important role in the growth of civilization. If man was to live at an altitude of 15,000 feet, he had to find a way to guarantee his food supply there. The answer lay in the cultivation of potatoes, *oca, ulluco,* and *quinoa* and the raising of llamas and alpacas—a combination that proved so productive, not only at the highest altitudes but also in the great basins around 9000-12,000 feet, that it put the spur to the budding population explosion. Similarly, the extreme aridity of the waterless desert required a special solution—in this case irrigation—which vastly multiplied the productivity of the land and the population it could support. The third extreme environment, the tropical rain forest, inspired a solution which, as we shall see, was not conducive to the growth of civilization.

Only a small part of the Andean countryside was useful to farmers and herders. The coastal valleys were separated by miles of waterless desert, the highlands valleys by rugged mountain masses. Large, uninterrupted stretches of farm land were available only in the major north-south highlands basins and on the Titicaca *altiplano.* At the same time, the distances between valley and valley were short enough that the inhabitants of one zone, though they traveled only on foot, had some knowledge of and contact with the people of neighboring zones.

The broken-up topography had several important effects. It concentrated the growing population into relatively small areas, within which special types of settlements, such as cities or dispersed communities, had to be worked out if dwellings were not to encroach on needed farm land. It set natural limits, both minimum and maximum, to the economic units integrated around irrigation systems. It restricted trade and communication, the expansion of which could only be achieved by a well-organized hierarchy controlling the labor force needed to build and maintain roads and bridges. And it provided semi-isolated environments in which the regional civilizations could develop their distinctive cultural patterns while benefiting from basic inventions that filtered in from other regions. These effects were most important on the coast, whereas the highlands probably always had a more open distribution of population centers and a freer flow of commodities and ideas.

FOOD PRODUCTION

An environment has advantages or disadvantages only in relation to the economy and technology of the people who occupy it. The relatively well-vegetated coast of 6000 B.C. barely sustained the small bands of food gatherers who lived in the *lomas*. Fishing and littoral harvesting, once adopted, were far more productive. Yet with irrigation and intensive agriculture, any of the larger coastal valleys supported more people than had lived on the entire coast in preceramic times. Except for the retreat of the *lomas*—which actually represented a decrease in the total resources of the area —and the clearing of the woods from the valleys, the physical environment of the coast did not undergo any significant changes, but with the succession of *lomas* gathering, littoral harvesting, and intensive agriculture, it behaved like three different environments.

Every civilization that has ever existed has been based on an agricultural economy, usually (in all cases except Mexico and the Maya area) coupled with animal husbandry. In Peru, in addition, fishing and shellfishing continued as important elements in the coastal economy throughout prehistoric times. The earliest temples and ceremonial centers on the central coast were built on the basis of a dominantly littoral food economy. Productive as the shore may have been, though, it set limits to the expansion and concentration of population and, therefore, to the elaboration of sociopolitical systems. These limits are well defined in the archaeological record, where we see the multiplication of small settlements within boundaries fixed by the number of good fishing sites, but where we do not find the growth of large settlements. The Peru Coastal Current could undoubtedly feed today's ten million Peruvians, but it could only do so if attacked by fleets of fishing boats and with the aid of modern systems of food preservation and distribution. The 50,000-100,000 persons who lived on the coast in Period VI probably represent the largest number that could be fed from the sea under aboriginal conditions.

Agriculture and animal husbandry, then, were the keys to the cities and empires of ancient Peru. They spurred the growth of the large, dense populations without which civilization would not have existed, and they were sufficiently productive that they allowed part of the population to produce food for all. The surplus economy made possible the social stratification and intensive specialization characteristic of Peruvian civilization by freeing large numbers of persons for activities other than food getting.

Peruvian food production had multiple origins. Maize, squash, common beans, jack beans, amaranth, avocados, and chili peppers all originated in Mexico or Central America. Cotton, at least one species of squash, *achira, pacae, guava, pepino, jíquima,* and *ciruela del fraile* all originated on the Andean coast, and sweet potatoes, lima beans, pineapples, *guanábana,* and *chirimoya* may first have been cultivated there. Cotton was as old in Mexico as in Peru, but the Peruvian species (*Gossypium barbadense*) was cultivated independently (see p. 76). Gourds were also grown very anciently in Mexico, but their constant association with cotton in Peru, even where other cultivated plants were absent, again suggests independent cultivation on the Andean coast. Plants of definite or probable highlands origin included *quinoa, cañihua, tarwi,* potatoes, *oca, ulluco, añu, lúcuma,* and *molle.* The tropical forest contributed manioc, coca, peanuts, and probably tobacco. Some of these Andean plants could have been first cultivated anywhere in Peru, Ecuador, or Colombia; others anywhere in Peru, western Bolivia, northern Chile, or northwestern Argentina. The llama and alpaca almost certainly were domesticated in the highlands of the southern area; the guinea pig and muscovy duck could have been domesticated anywhere in the Andes.

The earliest evidence of cultivation was in Period V on the central coast, where squash was grown at the Pampa site and cotton and gourds in the Encanto summer camps at Ancón and Chilca. One species of squash (*Cucurbita moschata*) at Pampa was of Mexican origin. When we know more about the history of Andean cultivation, we will probably find that the whole pattern was stimulated by the original introduction of squash from Meso-america, and that the native plants were cultivated only after the knowledge of farming techniques had been brought in from the north. On present evidence, however, it is possible that cotton and gourds were first cultivated independently on the southern coast before squash was brought in from the north; that the high-altitude complex of potatoes, *oca, ulluco, añu, quinoa,* and *cañihua* originated independently; and that manioc cultivation in the tropical lowlands may have represented yet a third such separate origin.

Whatever the role of the Mexican stimulus, the important things to note about Peruvian food production are its multiple origins and its multiple roles in the growth of civilization. We have already mentioned its functions in stimulating population growth and permitting stratification and specialization. Equally important is the fact that it led to the construction of irrigation systems.

The total acreage available for farming on the coast without irrigation was strictly limited. It consisted of narrow strips along each side of the rivers, and it probably could not have supported more than a tenth of the three million people who eventually lived in the coastal valleys. Beyond the immediate vicinity of the river, the water table dropped rapidly until, at the outer edges of the delta, it may have been as much as 100 feet below the surface of the ground. Mesquites can and did live in such an environment, but maize and squash and cotton cannot.

Irrigation served several purposes in ancient Peru: the expansion of farm land, the conservation of water through dry seasons, and the equitable distribution of water. The conformation of the coastal valleys was such that they never could have been irrigated efficiently with small ditches leading to individual plots. In order to downgrade a ditch sufficiently, it must be several miles long—scarcely an economical arrangement if the ditch is to water only one family's land. The only feasible solution—the one which was reached all over the coast in the Early Intermediate Period—was to take the water high up in the valley, run it through a few major canals, and distribute it to all of the farms through a network of ditches leading from the main canals. Once these canals were taking most of the water out of the rivers, their operation led to a further lowering of the water table, reduction of the summer flow in the lower parts of the rivers, and deliberate deforestation of the valleys to clear land in the areas reached by the new ditches and canals. The entire system, both main canals and secondary ditches, had to be cleaned once a year to keep the accumulated silt from blocking the flow of water.

The program of expanding farm land, the distribution of limited water resources, the clearing of the woods, and the upkeep of the irrigation systems all required a central authority capable of ordering the activity of every farmer in a given valley. Anyone who has observed a feud between modern Peruvian farmers over water rights or ditch-cleaning responsibilities will realize that the system could never have functioned on the basis of simple cooperation between families or settlements. The choice lay between a strong central government for each valley or economic disaster.

Present evidence indicates that the irrigation systems were not built until the requisite authority patterns had come into existence. The very existence of nucleated cities or ceremonial centers with monumental architecture implies a stratified and specialized socioeconomic and political system capable of running an irrigation system. In valley after valley, we find that either ceremonial centers or cities were built previous to the earliest dated irrigation system. All of the major irrigation systems date to the Early Intermediate Period; if any were begun earlier, we have no evidence of it. Yet ceremonial centers were found on the central coast starting in Preceramic Period VI, on the north-central coast in the Initial Period, and on the north coast in the Early Horizon. Similarly, cities were built in the Ica Valley late in the Early Horizon and were widespread on the south coast early in the Early Intermediate Period, whereas the south coastal irrigation systems were not built until late in the period.

We cannot, therefore, say that irrigation led to the centralization of authority but rather that, once authority was centralized, it became possible to build and maintain irrigation systems. Irrigation was thus a product of civilization, not a cause of it. Nevertheless, once the new farm lands were in use, irrigation became a fundamental fact of life which must have exerted considerable influence on the organization and continuity of the coastal states. When the population of any valley had expanded beyond the capacities of its original unirrigated acreage, the maintenance of the irrigation system became a matter of life or death. The dominance of ceremonial centers in the civilized north-central area during the Initial Period and Early Horizon, together with the religious nature of the Chavín diffusion, suggests that the earliest Peruvian states were theocratic in nature and had as their primary function the control of ritual. The exigencies of the irrigation systems, however, gave them a major secular function which gradually came to dominate all others.

Water control was never so important in the highlands as on the coast. Hillside terraces, which added minor amounts of farm land primarily dedicated to maize, had to be irrigated, and ditches were eventually also dug in the valley bottoms as a means of conserving water and overseeing its distribution. Though none of the highlands terraces and ditches—except those specifically built by the Incas—have been dated, it is probable that they were all quite late and that they represented lessons learned by the Huari and Inca conquerors from their coastal subjects. If so, irrigation in the highlands came about as a result of the imperialism of the great southern cities and cannot have played a significant part in the history of the highlands civilizations.

DEMOGRAPHY

The size and distribution of populations was the most important single factor in the growth of civilization. Large societies required complex systems of organization if they were to survive; small societies could not maintain any great degree of complexity in their organization, because they had neither the personnel to fill all of the different full-time roles of a complex organization nor the food-production capacity to feed many specialists. We define civilization primarily according to the complexity of its organization and the number and variety of its specialists. In a sense, the growth of civilization was a direct function of the growth of population. When there were too many people in a simple organization to allow it to function well, someone invented a new and more complex system capable of organizing larger numbers of people. If we can understand the causes of population growth and concentration, therefore, we can go a long way toward understanding the causes of civilization.

In the most general sense, population size is explained by some of the basic laws of biology: where there are abundant food and few natural enemies, populations grow; where food is scarce (relative to the size of the population) or natural enemies abundant, the population remains static or declines; given no change in food supply or natural enemies, an equilibrium is eventually reached and the population is stabilized at an optimum number for its particular environment. There are innumerable documented cases in which an animal population, finding itself in a new and favorable environment, has multiplied rapidly. There are also cases where such an expanding population has outstripped its food supply and been decimated by starvation in a series of bad years. Man, as an animal, is controlled by the same laws.

The *lomas* population of the Peruvian coast, in equilibrium with an unvarying food supply, did not change significantly within a period of nearly 5000 years. When the food supply shrank and man moved into the littoral environment, the available food increased many times over and so, immediately, did the population. That a new equilibrium was not soon reached was due to the fact that a still richer environment—the valleys awaiting cultivation—remained to be exploited. We do not have an example in Peru of population reduction due to growth beyond the limits of the food supply, but such cases are not unknown in human history. The classic Maya civilization of lowland Guatemala was destroyed and its territory almost depopulated because an ever-growing population ran up against an ever-shrinking productive capacity of the land.

There are two principal difficulties with the application of these laws to archaeological data: the estimation of population size and cultivated acreage at any given time, and the evaluation of the role of natural enemies. The difficulties of estimating population size in Peru, where quantitative analyses of midden components and the counting of contemporaneous houses have never been undertaken, have been pointed out in previous chapters. Agricultural practices have not changed much in many parts of modern Peru, so it should not be difficult to estimate the yield per acre of various crops in ancient times. When all the ditches of an ancient irrigation system can be traced out, it should be possible to determine the area of land under cultivation at a particular time in the past. Combining this information with the estimated yield and with a calculation of the relative quantity of various plant remains found in large-scale midden excavations, one could arrive at a realistic estimate of the acreage dedicated to different crops and, from this, an accurate picture of the total calories available to an ancient population. A partial study of this sort has been done in the Virú Valley.[5] For the rest of Peru, we are obliged to fall back on enlightened guesses and general statements, as this writer has done repeatedly in preceding pages.

Man faced no particular danger from large carnivores in Peru. Pumas and jaguars are fierce, but they are not notorious for their willingness to tangle with men. There are many stories of condors making off with babies, but most of them are just stories. The principal point of conflict between man and carnivore would have been the flocks of llamas and alpacas. The competition may have reduced the carnivore population, but it is not likely to have served as a brake on the human population.

It is doubtful, too, whether disease was a major factor in holding down population. Like all people before the rise of modern medical science, the ancient Peruvians had a high infant mortality rate and a relatively short life expectancy. The desert coast, however, is known for its freedom from endemic diseases other than a little malaria and those diseases that have accompanied modern industrialism and water pollution. Parasites are a problem at middle altitudes, but at the high altitudes a healthy climate again prevails. Miners may have suffered from silicosis, but, at least under the Incas, mining was not a full-time job. Syphilis is often said to have been a native Andean disease, and some Moche representations of mutilations are interpreted as the effects of syphilis, but I do not know that the case has been proved. The epidemics that decimated the Andean population in the sixteenth century were of European origin. Altogether, it was probably only in the *mon-*

---

[5] Willey, *Prehistoric Settlement Patterns,* pp. 394-95.

taña—where populations were never dense and civilization never developed—that disease was a significant limiting factor.

Man's most notorious natural enemy is man himself. The ancient Peruvians may not have been plagued by atom bombs and automobile fatalities, but, beginning in the Early Intermediate Period, they were involved in constant warfare. As we have seen (p. 121), warfare became prevalent in Peru at just about the time that large valley populations, cities, dispersed communities, and valley-wide states appeared in the record, and either coincident with or a little earlier than the building of the coastal irrigation systems. This clustering seems to mean that endemic warfare was due to pressure on the land. As agriculture expanded toward its natural limits, and especially after the irrigation systems were built, conflicts over land and water rights grew severe.

Sometimes war consisted of raids designed to destroy the enemy's power; settlements were looted and the victor withdrew without consolidating his victory. This was the situation, for example, in the south highlands during Late Intermediate times. In these cases, warfare may have served as a genuine deterrent to population growth because of the high mortality rate within whole populations. In many cases, however—the coastal states of the Early and Late Intermediate Periods, the Huari and Tiahuanaco Empires, and of course the Inca Empire—war was for conquest, and conquered territory was governed by the victor. In these cases the organized territories within the boundaries of the state were free of bloodshed. Unless there were incredibly high casualties among soldiers of breeding age—an unlikely event—the population would grow at a normal rate within the governed territories.

In some respects war served to spur the growth of civilization. Fortified cities like Marca Huamachuco and Kuelape, built for defensive purposes, concentrated formerly scattered rural populations into large, dense residential units within which both occupational specialization and government would quickly have become major factors in the life of the people. Similarly, conquest warfare led to the expansion of states and demanded more elaborate and sophisticated organizations to cope with the large number of people being governed.

TRADE AND COMMUNICATION

Most ancient civilizations grew up on the basis of a broad network of trade within which goods and ideas flowed freely from region to region. Peru was unusual in that, with brief exceptions, long-range commerce was more restricted than in ancient Mexico or the Near East. Except for the obsidian trade in the south, which lasted from preceramic times through the Early Intermediate Period, and perhaps commerce in tin and copper from south to north, raw materials seem to have circulated only within limited regions. Food, except for such delicacies as fresh fish for the Inca emperor, was strictly a local matter, each valley or region living off what it produced. Within a given region, however, there was a smoothly functioning trade between different ecological zones: fish for farm produce, high altitude crops for low. Some plant and animal products traveled farther. Coca was traded from the *montaña* to the highlands and coast, cotton moved uphill, alpaca wool moved downhill. Monkeys were imported from the *montaña* to the coast, apparently as pets.

Most long-range trade, however, took the form of small quantities of high-quality manufactured goods that moved from region to region as luxury items for the upper classes. The trade in fine pottery is best known, but textiles and ornamental metal work followed the same routes. The Peruvian luxury trade was unusual in the way it periodically expanded and contracted, following the alternate unification and regionalization of Peruvian culture. There is no trace of an interregional luxury trade in preceramic times or in the Initial Period. With the spread of the Chavín cult we find fancy trade pottery circulating throughout Chavín territory and between the central and south coast, but we do not know whether the south highlands entered into commercial relations with the rest of Peru during the Early Horizon. After a reduction in scope during the Early Intermediate Period, we again find the luxury trade flourishing under the Huari Empire, with the Viñaque, Pachacamac, and Cajamarca III styles especially favored by the upper classes over a very large area. The volume of trade diminished in the Late Intermediate Period, though some specimens of the Soniche and Chimú styles traveled far from home.

Finally, the luxury trade reached an all-time peak in volume and range under the Incas.

In ancient Mexico, control of the luxury trade was one of the major functions of government. We do not know that it had such importance in Peru, but the evidence of trade is nevertheless important for several reasons. For one thing, it shows the degree to which, at any given time, the upper classes of different regions were in contact with each other. For another, it is a measure of the unification achieved during periods of empire. In addition it serves to mark out the routes and times of diffusion, because the flow of ideas has always tended to follow that of goods.

Throughout most of prehistory, the various regions of Peru were self-contained and self-subsistent, related to each other only through a minimum of trade and through border skirmishes. Only during the early part of each horizon, when the spread of a cult or empire actively unified a large area, were the lines of trade and communication fully open. The individual regions were never entirely cut off from their neighbors, of course. Both stylistic ideas and basic inventions moved from region to region even at periods of maximum isolation. The archaeological evidence, however, indicates that, beginning with the Early Horizon, the major flow of innovations across Peru took place during the periods of unification. Before the Early Horizon, basic inventions spread gradually from settlement to settlement. Afterward, the Chavín, Huari, Tiahuanaco, Chimú, and Inca peoples carried them rapidly across large areas.

Important as were the periods of unification, those of regionalization were no less significant. Nothing stimulates invention like new ideas; the cults and empires not only spread technological and social innovations, but also, by doing so, put the spur to new inventions. The intermediate periods, in turn, were times when new ideas were modified to fit the regional cultural patterns. They guaranteed a diversity of ideas to be spread during the periods of unification.

One outstanding characteristic of civilizations is the fact that they have not grown in a vacuum, with the important innovations all spreading out from a single center. Rather, the multiplicity of inventive centers is so universal in the history of civilization that we may consider it an essential part of the process. Civilization may be carried more or less intact into new areas, but it has only developed in fairly large areas containing numerous sources of basic ideas. We have already mentioned the multiple origins of Peruvian agriculture, which involved centers of innovation as far away as Mexico and the tropical forest of lowlands South America. Pottery making came from the northern Andes, temples and ceremonial centers from the central coast, gold metallurgy from the north, copper and bronze from the south, cities from the south, irrigation from the coast, dressed stone architecture from the highlands. The earliest states seem to have been coastal, whereas the first round of empire originated in the southern highlands and the second on the north coast.

Together with this multiplicity of centers, we find that the focus of innovation and of power shifted from region to region during the course of Peruvian prehistory. During Preceramic Period VI and the Initial Period, dense populations, temples, and ceremonial centers were all concentrated in north-central Peru. During this time, about 2000-900 B.C., the term "civilization" was only applicable to the coastal valleys from Casma to Lurín and to highlands centers in the Callejón de Huaylas and the upper Huallaga. This trend peaked early in the Early Horizon with the spread of the Chavín cult. Thereafter, the focus of power shifted southward until, in the Middle Horizon, the great cities of the southern highlands dominated the country militarily, politically, and culturally. Whatever the reason for the fall of Huari and Tiahuanaco, the destruction of their empires left a power vacuum which was to be occupied successively by the kings of Chanchan in the north and Cuzco in the south. Where the next focus might have been we will never know; with the fall of the Incas the scepter passed to the kings of Castille and the native Andean peoples went into an eclipse that has lasted to the present day.

The importance of multiple centers and shifting foci lay in the cultural variety they provided. The growth of civilization depended on the appearance and successful diffusion of many basic technological and social inventions. Inventions, however, are neither made nor diffused in static situations. The greater the fund of cultural variety, the greater is the likelihood that significant inventions will be made; the more people are accustomed to change, the easier is the process of diffusion of techniques and systems from one society to another. Peruvian civilization could probably never have come into existence were it not for the multiplicity of its origins.

SETTLEMENT PATTERNS

Maps 11-14 summarize the history of ceremonial centers and cities in ancient Peru. The early large temples and ceremonial centers of the north-central region—Río Seco, Chuquitanta, La Florida, the terraced structure at Ancón, Las Haldas, the Haldas temple at Culebras, Toril, and Kotosh—represent the earliest monumental buildings of any kind known in the Americas. They were probably all built between 2000 and 1500 B.C. They give evidence of a well-developed pattern of public ritual, an economy of sufficient abundance to free a good deal of labor from subsistence activities, and a measure of social stratification and specialization. They show, too, that it was in the north-central region, both coast and highlands, that civilization first developed in Peru. They were built at a time of fairly light population densities and on the basis of a mixed economy in which, on the coast, littoral harvesting played a greater role than did farming. They have no obvious ecological explanation, and I am unwilling, at this point, to venture a guess as to why these great early centers were built.

The Chavín diffusion carried ceremonial centers—and with them civilization—throughout the northern half of Peru (Map 11). Late in the Early Horizon, we see the first scattered evidences of settlements large enough to be called cities.

Both cities and ceremonial centers reached their apogee in the Early Intermediate Period, the former in the south and the latter in the north (Map 12). Civilization had spread by this time to all of Peru except the *montaña* (where it never took root) and the far south coast. A fundamental change also took place in the synchoritic systems of the northern ceremonial centers, at least on the coast. The earlier centers had served as the focal points in a society composed of villages and rural towns built along the shore and in the valley bottoms. During the Early Intermediate Period

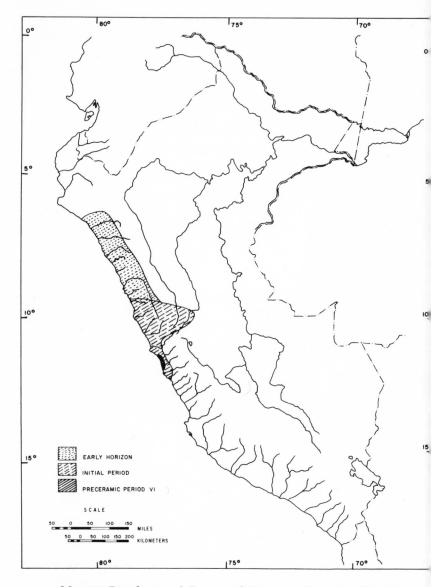

MAP 11. Distribution of Ceremonial Centers in Preceramic Period VI, the Initial Period, and the Early Horizon

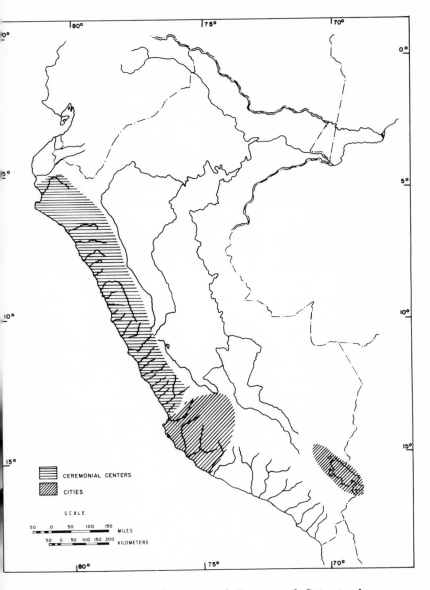

MAP 12. Distribution of Ceremonial Centers and Cities in the Early Intermediate Period

the village pattern faded out in most of the coastal valleys and was replaced by the dispersed community pattern, which was adapted to the topography of the unwatered land along the edges of the valleys. This change was associated with the construction of the irrigation systems and the need to maximize farm land by removing the settlements to infertile areas.

The new organization of settlements in the north and the growth of cities in the south can be understood as results of the continuing population explosion and the need to extend the cultivated areas that fed them. In the north, the population was removed from the arable land; in the south, large numbers of people were concentrated into relatively small zones (cities) in order to free the greatest possible area for cultivation. The cities probably concentrated all of the functions of government, religion, manufacture, and commerce into single large centers. Government and religion had their seats in the northern ceremonial centers, but craft centers and markets were probably located elsewhere within the dispersed communities.

With the conquest of northern Peru by Huari, cities rapidly replaced the old ceremonial centers (Map 13). Some of the cities may have been built by the conquerors, others by the local rulers in imitation of Huari. Some, such as Marca Huamachuco, were built for defensive purposes. For the most part the cities were new settlements and were not located on the sites of the old ceremonial centers, which suggests that the old priest-rulers had gone into oblivion and that the cities were built and occupied by a new ruling class. Pachacamac was an exception: it had been a ceremonial center in the Early Intermediate Period, and the Middle Horizon city grew up around the old temples.

With the fall of Huari and Tiahuanaco, urbanism came to an end in the south, though it now flourished as never before in the north (Map 14). Except for an occasional ceremonial center like Tacaraca in the Ica Valley, there is little architectural evidence of civilization in the south during the Late Intermediate Period. Not until the Late Horizon, when Pachacuti rebuilt Cuzco, was there any settlement in southern Peru which might deserve the name of city.

Once the ancient populations neared their maximum size, the

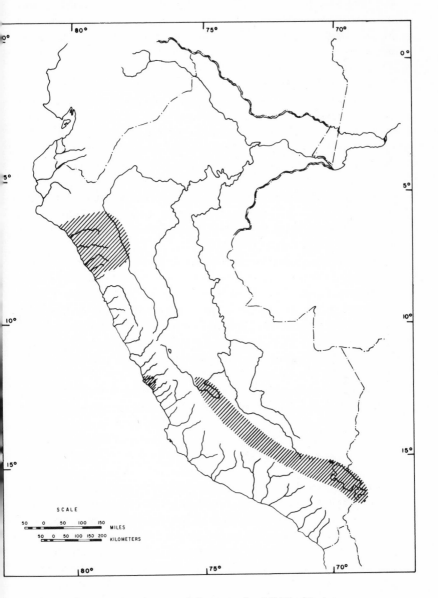

MAP 13. Distribution of Cities in the Middle Horizon

city-town-village system and the ceremonial center-dispersed community system were the two principal organizations of settlements in the civilized parts of the country. At any given time they were found in mutually exclusive areas, though there are a few cases of cities coexisting with ceremonial centers and one case (the north coast in the Late Intermediate Period) when cities and dispersed communities existed side by side. For the most part, these two organizational systems represented separate solutions to the same set of problems. Only rarely can we find a ceremonial center that grew into a city or a city that evolved into a ceremonial center through loss of its resident population. The outstanding exception was Pachacamac, where the importance of the oracle guaranteed continued occupation and prestige. Under the urban Huari influence, the old ceremonial center there grew into a city; under the more rural Incas, it shrank back to the status of ceremonial center.

Nor can we say that one settlement system or the other was more effective in dominating ancient Peru. The first and second rounds of empire, in the Middle Horizon and Late Intermediate Period, originated in the great cities respectively of the southern highlands and the north coast. But the third and greatest round, that of the Incas, was rural in concept and rural in origin. Map 14 shows Cuzco as a city, but it could equally well be conceived as an unusual type of ceremonial center (see p. 162). If it was a city, it was the only one the Incas ever built. Any other Late Horizon city represents local tradition which the Incas decided not to interfere with.

SPECIALIZATION AND STRATIFICATION

Cities, ceremonial centers and dispersed communities are best seen as results rather than as causes of the broad trends of food production, population growth, and interregional trade. Once built, however, either a city or a ceremonial center must have had a considerable effect on the organization of society. Even the most achoritic city must have contained many specialists, and ceremonial centers were totally specialized. Specialists required the support of the peasantry and could support their demands both through force

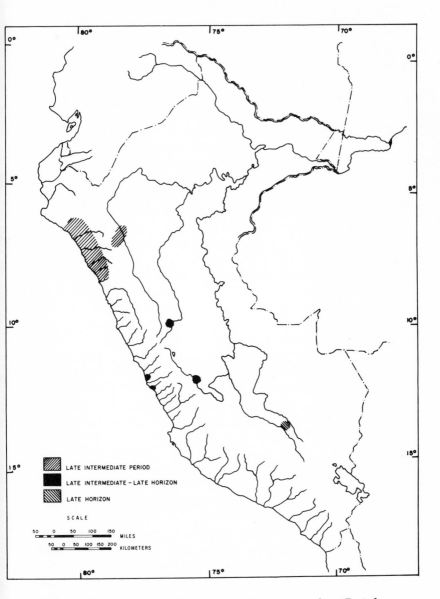

MAP 14. Distribution of Cities in the Late Intermediate Period
and the Late Horizon

and by supplying the rural population with indispensable goods and services. The network of relationships thus established must soon have become so deeply embedded in the fabric of society that it could seldom be broken even by the radical changes brought by successive conquests.

Social stratification went hand in hand with specialization in ancient Peru. Wherever there is evidence of specialists, there is evidence that some of them constituted an upper class that ruled society. Specialization and stratification formed a self-reinforcing system. Bureaucracy always breeds new bureaucrats. Class privileges are defended by increasing the social distance between classes. The products and services of specialists become ever more essential as the food-producing class forgets the techniques and skills of self-subsistence. Once an ancient society was diversified, diversification became a fact of life without which the society could not continue to exist.

Once the basic class system was established, it had an important effect on the flow of goods and ideas. Neither independent village farmers nor the peasantry in the civilized societies had much contact with nor knowledge of people who were not their immediate neighbors. The upper classes, however, had more wide-ranging interest in and knowledge of the sociopolitical world around them. Their very existence fostered the luxury trade and threw open new avenues for the spread of ideas across the whole of ancient Peru.

The structure of Peruvian civilization—urban-rural, ruler-ruled, specialist-food producer—was broken once, midway through the Middle Horizon. The effect of the break was the fall of empires, the destruction of cities, and the almost permanent ruralization of the entire southern half of Peru.

THE LIMITS OF PERUVIAN CIVILIZATION

The Tiahuanaco Empire incorporated much of northern Chile and of Bolivia south of the Titicaca basin; the Incas extended these conquests southward to the Maule River and into northwestern Argentina. This southern area is one in which limited agriculture and animal husbandry may have been practiced at a quite early date, but to which pottery, village life, and copper metallurgy did not diffuse until the beginning of the Early Intermediate Period. Except for their integration into the two empires, there is no reason to consider that the people of northern Chile and Argentina were ever civilized. Their populations were neither very dense nor organized around cities or ceremonial centers. Except when they were under foreign dominance, there is no evidence that they had any marked degree of either specialization (other than metallurgy) or stratification. There is one fundamental difference in the southern environment that is sufficient to explain the lack of an indigenous civilization: it did not have enough water to support either a large population or any great degree of specialization. Northern Chile constitutes the world's driest desert, and the northwestern Argentine region is scarcely rainier. Where the scant water does not sink into the sand or drain into infertile salt pans, it usually runs in deep canyons that are useless for irrigation. Native civilization was impossible under such circumstances, because it could not develop the necessary economic base.

If the southern marches were too dry, the *montaña* on the east was too wet. Upper Amazonia is notorious for its shallow, acid, easily leached soils and frequent inundations. It could be farmed only by the swidden system, clearing fields by cutting and burning, planting without turning the soil. Fields lost their fertility through leaching in a year or two and had to be left fallow for many years until they were reclaimed by forest vegetation. Since lands around a village were often exhausted before any of them had recuperated, villages were occasionally moved in search of new land to clear. Large settlements like the Andean towns and cities could not exist under such circumstances, nor could the population of any region ever grow very large. Civilization requires the concentration of population, but the *montaña* environment led to scattered populations and dispersed settlements. Only rarely and under exceptionally favorable circumstances has civilization developed in tropical forests; it was impossible in the Peruvian *montaña*. Not only did the native peoples of the area fail to develop civilization. The Incas failed to import their own civilization to the *montaña*, the Spanish failed in their turn, and the modern Peruvians have failed in spite of repeated attempts.

The southern and eastern limits of ancient Peruvian civilization were thus natural boundaries defined by environmental conditions. This is not true of the northern border. Ecuadorean highlands valleys may have been somewhat smaller and more separated than those of Peru, but they were not less fertile. Further north, the Magdalena and Cauca Valleys of Colombia, which run from the Caribbean coast for hundreds of miles up into the highlands, were among the best farm land on the continent, as was the Guayas Basin of Ecuador. As we would expect, the ancient cultures of the northern Andes showed some of the characteristics of civilization, including economies based on food production, social stratification, and, in the Magdalena Valley, small local states competing for dominance. Populations were smaller than in Peru, however; there was little monumental architecture, cities and ceremonial centers were absent, metallurgists and local kings were almost the only specialists, and—except for the Inca conquest of Ecuador—there were no empires.

The northern Andes took an early lead in pottery making, as we have seen, and the early diffusion of Mesoamerican cultivated plants must have come down through western Colombia and Ecuador. Thereafter, however, the northern Andean area was largely cut off from the development of civilization. To the south, there was a cultural barrier, inexplicable but real, between Ecuador and Peru. After the diffusion of pottery making, only an occasional artifact type or stylistic idea filtered through the barrier until the Incas broke it down.

To the north, the rain forest of Panama and southern Central America was nearly as impropitious for civilization as upper Amazonia. It isolated Colombia on the north from the developments taking place in Mexico and the Maya area. The sea route was open, of course, especially on the Pacific coast. Commercial rafting brought many Mesoamerican culture traits to the coasts of Ecuador and southern Colombia, whence they moved up the Guayas Basin or directly into the highlands of Colombia. For the most part, however, these traits consisted of stylistic ideas or luxury items which had no bearing on the growth of civilization.

One reason that civilization did not develop in Ecuador and Colombia, then, is that they were isolated from the flow of basic innovations. Another reason may lie in the relative inhospitality of the coastal environment and the lack of the interplay between coast and highlands which was so important in the growth of Peruvian civilization. The southern coast of Ecuador was almost as dry as the Peruvian coast, and it lacked the permanent rivers that made irrigation possible in Peru. The northern coast of Ecuador and the Pacific coast of Colombia were tropical and rainy, lined with mangrove swamps and covered with jungles. These conditions grow worse as one goes northward until, in northern Colombia, one finds the heaviest rainfall and the most impenetrable forests in all of South America. Intensive agriculture, therefore, was possible only around the Gulf of Guayaquil and in the zone of transition between desert and rain forest, and irrigation was never developed. Without the dialogue between coast and highlands, the latter area also failed to develop irrigation on any meaningful scale. Thus, though the land was potentially as rich as that of Peru, agriculture was less productive and populations fell into equilibrium with their food supply rather than continuing to increase and concentrate. It is probable, therefore, that the northern Andes did not develop civilization because of barriers to communication and because of the unfavorable environment of an essential part of the area.

CONCLUSION

Peruvian civilization grew up in an extreme environment which, in spite of its rigors, offered rich rewards to men who brought the right technology to it. Agriculture seems to have spread into Peru from the north, stimulating the cultivation of many useful native plants and enormously increasing the productivity of the valleys of both coast and highlands. With the addition of irrigation and of animal husbandry—the one invented on the coast, the other probably originating in the highlands—and the retention of fishing and littoral harvesting, both the desert and the high plateaus contributed to the general fruitfulness. Maize, potatoes, manioc, guinea pigs, and llamas, all raised on extremely fertile land, gave rise to a rapid growth of population. The Peruvian topography concentrated many people into relatively small areas, making complex organizations and special settlement patterns necessary to insure prosperity. These new organizations took the form of states, cities, and the ceremonial center—dispersed community pattern. Social stratification and specialization grew up along with the new types of organization. Once established, they became necessary to the functioning of the system and thus reinforced the snowballing process of the growth of civilization.

Commerce and the interchange of ideas were also essential parts of the development of Peruvian civilization. The luxury trade linked up the ancient societies at the top level. Basic inventions, such as irrigation and copper and bronze metallurgy, were made in different parts of the country and were spread along the routes established by trading. Conquest, too, served not only to expand the states but also to spread such fundamentals as cities and bronze tools. All of these factors—environment, food production, dense populations, specialization, stratification, special settlement patterns, trade, diffusion, and conquest warfare—contributed to the growth of Peruvian civilization. The geographical limits of native civilization were set by the lack of water to the south, of population concentration to the east, and of irrigation and open communications to the north.

We should not, of course, lose sight of individual achievements. Pachacuti and Topa Inca were brilliant organizers, and their generals were great leaders within the tactical tradition of Andean warfare. Without these men, Inca history would not have followed the course that it did. Undoubtedly there were other geniuses in earlier periods who made the right inventions at the right times or whose achievements in public life reshaped their societies. Individual genius, however, is not amenable to archaeological study and is not necessary to the explanation of culture history. Explanation lies in delimiting the circumstances that surrounded a trend of cultural change and identifying the factors shaping the change and the interacting processes of which it was composed. By doing this for prehistoric Peru, we can reach an understanding, not of the genius of individuals, but of the genius of the Andean peoples as a whole.

Bibliography

The following list is highly selective with special emphasis on books published since 1950 and on those dealing with subjects stressed in this book. Most of the older classics of Peruvian archaeology have been omitted, as have countless more recent articles. For the reader who wishes to examine more fully the literature of Peruvian archaeology, the following works all contain bibliographic references. For a particularly exhaustive bibliography, see Mason, *Ancient Civilizations*.

GENERAL

BENNETT, WENDELL C., and JUNIUS BIRD, *Andean Culture History*. Handbook Series, No. 15. New York: American Museum of Natural History, 1949.

BUSHNELL, G. H. S., *Peru*, Ancient Peoples and Places. London: Thames and Hudson, 1956.

COLLIER, DONALD, "Development of Civilization on the Coast of Peru," *Social Science Monographs*, I, 19-27. Washington, D.C.: Pan American Union, 1955.

GROBMAN, ALEXANDER, et al., *Races of Maize in Peru, their Origins, Evolution and Classification*, National Research Council, Publication No. 915. Washington, D. C.: National Academy of Sciences, 1961.

KROEBER, ALFRED L., *Peruvian Archaeology in 1942*, Viking Fund Publications in Anthropology, No. 4. New York: The Viking Fund, Inc., 1944.

MASON, J. ALDEN, *The Ancient Civilizations of Peru*, Pelican Books A395. Harmondsworth, Middlesex: Penguin Books Ltd., 1957.

MENZEL, DOROTHY, "Style and Time in the Middle Horizon," *Ñawpa Pacha*, II (1964), 1-105.

ROWE, JOHN H., "Urban Settlements in Ancient Peru," *Ñawpa Pacha*, I (1963), 1-27.

TELLO, JULIO C., "Discovery of the Chavín Culture in Peru," *American Antiquity*, IX, No. 1 (1943), 135-60.

TOWLE, MARGARET A., *The Ethnobotany of Pre-Columbian Peru*, Viking Fund Publications in Anthropology, No. 30. New York: Wenner-Gren Foundation for Anthropological Research, Inc., 1961.

PRECERAMIC

BIRD, JUNIUS B., "Preceramic Cultures in Chicama and Virú," in *A Reappraisal of Peruvian Archaeology*, ed. Wendell C. Bennett. Memoirs of the Society for American Archaeology, No. 4, 21-28. Menasha, Wis., 1948.

CARDICH, AUGUSTO, *Lauricocha, Fundamentos para una Prehistoria de los Andes Centrales*, Studia Praehistorica III. Buenos Aires: Centro Argentino de Estudios Prehistóricos, 1964.

ENGEL, FRÉDÉRIC, "Sites et Établissements sans Céramique de la Côte Peruvienne," *Journal de la Société des Américanistes*, Nouvelle Série, XLVI (1957), 67-155.

———, *A Preceramic Settlement on the Central Coast of Peru: Asia, Unit 1*, Transactions of the American Philosophical Society, LIII, Part 3. Philadelphia, 1963.

KELLEY, DAVID H., and DUCCIO BONAVÍA, "New Evidence for Preceramic Maize on the Coast of Peru," *Ñawpa Pacha*, I (1963), 39-41.

LANNING, EDWARD P., "Early Man in Peru," *Scientific American*, CCXIII, No. 4 (1965), 68-76.

FAR NORTH COAST

Izumi, Seiichi, and Kazuo Terada, *Andes 3, Excavations at Pechiche and Garbanzal, Tumbes Valley, Peru.* Tokyo: Kadokawa Publishing Co., 1966.

Lanning, Edward P., *A Ceramic Sequence for the Piura and Chira Coast, North Peru,* University of California Publications in American Archaeology and Ethnology, XLVI, No. 2. Berkeley and Los Angeles: University of California Press, 1963.

NORTH COAST

Bennett, Wendell C., *The Gallinazo Group, Virú Valley, Peru,* Yale University Publications in Anthropology, No. 43. New Haven: Yale University Press, 1950.

Collier, Donald, *Cultural Chronology and Change as Reflected in the Ceramics of the Virú Valley, Peru,* Fieldiana: Anthropology, Vol. XLIII. Chicago: Chicago Natural History Museum, 1955.

Larco Hoyle, Rafael, *Cronología Arqueológica del Norte del Perú.* Trujillo: Hacienda Chiclín, 1948.

Rowe, John H., "The Kingdom of Chimor," *Acta Americana,* VI, Nos. 1-2 (1948), 26-59.

Schaedel, Richard P., "Major Ceremonial and Population Centers in Northern Peru," in *The Civilizations of Ancient America,* ed. Sol Tax. Selected Papers of the XXIXth International Congress of Americanists, I, 232-43. Chicago: The University of Chicago Press, 1951.

Strong, William Duncan, and Clifford Evans, Jr., *Cultural Stratigraphy in the Virú Valley, Northern Peru,* Columbia Studies in Archeology and Ethnology, Vol. IV. New York: Columbia University Press, 1952.

Willey, Gordon R., *Prehistoric Settlement Patterns in the Virú Valley, Peru,* Bureau of American Ethnology, Bulletin 155. Washington, D.C.: Smithsonian Institution, 1953.

NORTH-CENTRAL COAST

Collier, Donald, "Archaeological Investigations in the Casma Valley, Peru," in *Akten des 34. Internationalen Amerikanistenkongresses,* pp. 411-17. Wien, 1962.

Tello, Julio C., *Arqueología del Valle de Casma, Culturas: Chavín, Santa o Huaylas Yunga y Sub-Chimú*, Publicación Antropológica del Archivo "Julio C. Tello," Vol. I. Lima: Universidad Nacional Mayor de San Marcos, 1956.

CENTRAL COAST

Jijón y Caamaño, Jacinto, *Maranga, Contribución al Conocimiento de los Aborigenes del Valle del Rimac*. Quito: La Prensa Católica, 1949.

Kroeber, Alfred L., *Proto-Lima: a Middle Period Culture of Peru*, Fieldiana: Anthropology, Vol. XLIV, No. 1. Chicago: Chicago Natural History Museum, 1954.

Lanning, Edward P., "An Early Ceramic Style from Ancón, Central Coast of Peru," *Ñawpa Pacha*, I (1963), 47-59.

Patterson, Thomas C., and Edward P. Lanning, "Changing Settlement Patterns on the Central Peruvian Coast," *Ñawpa Pacha*, II (1964), 113-23.

Strong, William Duncan, et al., *Archeological Studies in Peru, 1941-1942*, Columbia Studies in Archeology and Ethnology, Vol. I. New York: Columbia University Press, 1943.

Tabío, Ernesto E., *Excavaciones en Playa Grande, Costa Central del Perú*, Arqueológicas, Publicación del Instituto de Investigaciones Antropológicas, No. 1. Lima: Museo Nacional de Antropología y Arqueología, 1957.

Willey, Gordon R., and John M. Corbett, *Early Ancón and Early Supe Culture*, Columbia Studies in Archeology and Ethnology, Vol. III. New York: Columbia University Press, 1954.

SOUTH-CENTRAL COAST

Kroeber, Alfred L., *Archaeological Explorations in Peru, Part IV, Cañete Valley*, Anthropology Memoirs, Vol. II, No. 4. Chicago: Field Museum of Natural History, 1937.

Wallace, Dwight T., "Early Horizon Ceramics in the Cañete Valley of Peru," *Ñawpa Pacha*, I (1963), 35-38.

SOUTH COAST

BELLINGER, LOUISA, and JUNIUS B. BIRD, *Paracas Fabrics and Nazca Needlework*. Washington, D.C.: National Publishing Co., 1954.

KROEBER, ALFRED L., *Toward Definition of the Nazca Style*, University of California Publications in American Archaeology and Ethnology, Vol. XLIII, No. 4. Berkeley and Los Angeles: University of California Press, 1956.

MENZEL, DOROTHY, "The Inca Occupation of the South Coast of Peru," *Southwestern Journal of Anthropology*, XV, No. 2 (1959), 125-42.

————, et al., *The Paracas Pottery of Ica: a Study in Style and Time*, University of California Publications in American Archaeology and Ethnology, Vol. L. Berkeley and Los Angeles: University of California Press, 1964.

ROARK, RICHARD P., "From Monumental to Proliferous in Nasca Pottery," *Ñawpa Pacha*, III (1965), 1-92.

ROOT, WILLIAM C., "The Metallurgy of the Southern Coast of Peru," *American Antiquity*, XV, No. 1 (1949), 10-17.

ROWE, JOHN H., "La Arqueología de Ica," *Revista de la Facultad de Letras de la Universidad Nacional "San Luis Gonzaga" de Ica*, Año I (1962), 113-21.

STRONG, WILLIAM DUNCAN, *Paracas, Nazca and Tiahuanacoid Cultural Relationships in South Coastal Peru*, Memoirs of the Society for American Archaeology, No. 13. Salt Lake City, 1957.

TELLO, JULIO C., *Paracas, Primera Parte*. Lima: Empresa Gráfica T. Scheuch S.A., 1959.

MIDDLE MARAÑON

McCOWN, THEODORE D., *Pre-Incaic Huamachuco; Survey and Excavations in the Northern Sierra of Peru*, University of California Publications in American Archaeology and Ethnology, Vol. XXXIX, No. 4. Berkeley and Los Angeles: University of California Press, 1945.

REICHLEN, HENRI, and PAULE REICHLEN, "Recherches Archéologiques dans les Andes de Cajamarca," *Journal de la Société des Américanistes*, Nouvelle Série, XXXVIII (1949), 137-74.

CALLEJÓN DE HUAYLAS AND CHAVÍN DE HUÁNTAR

Bennett, Wendell C., *The North Highlands of Peru*, Anthropological Papers, Vol. XXXIX, Part 1. New York: American Museum of Natural History, 1944.

Rowe, John H., *Chavín Art, an Inquiry into its Form and Meaning*. New York: The Museum of Primitive Art, 1962.

Tello, Julio C., *Chavín, Cultura Matriz de la Civilización Andina, Primera Parte*, Publicación Antropológica del Archivo "Julio C. Tello," Vol. II. Lima: Universidad Nacional Mayor de San Marcos, 1956.

HUALLAGA BASIN

Izumi, Seiichi, and Toshihiko Sono, *Andes 2, Excavations at Kotosh, Peru, 1963*. Tokyo: Kadokawa Publishing Co., 1963.

Lathrap, Donald W., and Lawrence Roys, "The Archaeology of the Cave of the Owls in the Upper Montaña of Peru," *American Antiquity*, XXIX, No. 1 (1963), 27-38.

UCAYALI BASIN

Lathrap, Donald W., "The Cultural Sequence at Yarinacocha, Eastern Peru," American Antiquity, XXIII, No. 4 (1958), 379-88.

MANTARO BASIN

Bennett, Wendell C., *Excavations at Wari, Ayacucho, Peru*, Yale University Publications in Anthropology, No. 49. New Haven: Yale University Press, 1953.

Lumbreras, Luis Guillermo, "La Cultura de Wari, Ayacucho," *Etnología y Arqueología*, Año I, No. 1 (1960), 130-227. Lima: Instituto de Etnología y Arqueología, Facultad de Letras, Universidad Nacional Mayor de San Marcos.

URUBAMBA BASIN

Rowe, John H., *An Introduction to the Archaeology of Cuzco*, Papers of the Peabody Museum of American Archaeology and Ethnology,

Vol. XXVII, No. 2. Cambridge: Harvard University Press, 1944.

———, "Archaeological Explorations in Southern Peru, 1954-55," *American Antiquity*, XXII, No. 2 (1956), 135-51.

TITICACA BASIN

KIDDER, ALFRED, II, *Some Early Sites in the Northern Lake Titicaca Basin*, Papers of the Peabody Museum of American Archaeology and Ethnology, Vol. XXXVII, No. 1. Cambridge: Harvard University Press, 1943.

PONCE SANGINES, CARLOS, *Descripción Sumaria del Templete Semisubterráneo de Tiwanaku*, Publicación No. 2 del Centro de Investigaciones Arqueológicas en Tiwanaku. Tiahuanaco, 1964.

RYDÉN, STIG, *Archaeological Researches in the Highlands of Bolivia*. Göteborg: Elanders Boktryckeri Aktiebolag, 1947.

———, *Andean Excavations*, The Ethnographical Museum of Sweden, Monograph Series, Publications No. 4, 6. Stockholm: Elanders Boktryckeri Aktiebolag, 1957, 1959.

TSCHOPIK, MARION H., *Some Notes on the Archaeology of the Department of Puno, Peru*, Papers of the Peabody Museum of American Archaeology and Ethnology, Vol. XXVII, No. 3. Cambridge: Harvard University Press, 1946.

Glossary

Achoritic: (A settlement) lacking a dependent rural population.

Agglutination: Concentration of houses and other structures into a compact settlement.

Artifact: Any tool, weapon, ornament or other object which owes its form to manufacture or use.

Assemblage: Collection of artifact forms characteristic of the culture of a particular region and time span.

Association: Relationship between archaeological sites, artifacts, natural features, etc.

Biface: Large, heavy stone tool, chipped on both faces, characteristic of the Chivateros 1 and 2 Complexes.

Blade: A long, narrow flake with parallel sides.

Burin: Stone tool with a chisel-like point made by striking one or more long chips off the side edge.

Carbon 14: Radioactive isotope of carbon, the decay of which is measured to determine its age.

Ceremonial Center: Complex of monumental public buildings with few or no permanent residents.

Chicha: Beer made of maize, *oca,* etc.

Chipping: Technique of manufacturing stone artifacts by striking or pressing off pieces until the form is achieved.

Coiling: Technique of manufacturing pottery by building up the vessel with ropelike coils of clay.

Complex (architectural): An organized group of buildings making up a settlement or a unit within a settlement.

Complex (cultural): Total of cultural forms (artifact assemblage, settlement pattern, food economy, etc.) characteristic of a particular region and time span.

Core: Block of stone from which flakes have been struck.

Core Tool: Core that has been shaped or used as a tool.

Culture: Total way of life, in general or of a given people at a particular time. In archaeology, the restricted meaning ("a culture") is almost synonymous with "complex," though it is used somewhat more broadly and loosely.

Curaca: Administrative official in the Inca Empire.

Denticulate: Stone tool with a ragged, sawlike edge.

Dispersed Community: Settlement, usually without clearly defined boundaries, in which residential units are scattered over a large area rather than concentrated together.

Embossing: Technique of decorating metal in which the design is pressed out over a soft anvil.

Flake: Piece of stone struck off from a larger block (core). Either the flake or the core, or both, can be shaped into artifacts.

Gauze: Cloth with openwork patterns made by manipulating the warps.

Heddle: Device on a loom used to raise and lower alternate warps, permitting the weft to be shot through in a straight line.

Ikat: Textile technique in which the design is dyed on the warps before weaving.

Kenning: Visual metaphor (e.g., hair represented as snakes) characteristic of the Chavín style.

Lomas: Areas of vegetation supported by condensation from fog rather than by rainfall.

Looping: Technique of manufacturing textiles in which a single element—rather than separate warps and wefts—is interlaced without knotting.

"Lost Wax": Metallurgical technique in which the molten metal replaces a wax lining in a hollow mold.

Midden: Refuse dump.

Milling Stone: Large flat stone on which seeds are ground with a smaller stone held in one hand.

Montaña: The forested eastern slopes of the Andes.

Nucleation: Presence, in a settlement, of a central area of public buildings.

Paddle-and-Anvil: Technique of manufacturing pottery in which the vessel is hammered into shape with a flat paddle, the blows of which are absorbed by a cobblestone held inside the vessel.

Pampa: Any flat land, in *Quechua*.

Pectoral: Ornament worn on the chest.

Percussion Flaking: Chipping technique in which flakes are struck off, usually by a cobblestone hammer.

Pleistocene: Geological period ending about 10,000 years ago, characterized by repeated advances of continental glaciers.

Prehistory: In any given area, the span of human existence before the invention or introduction of writing.

Press Molding: Technique of manufacturing pottery by pressing plastic clay into partial molds, after which the parts of the vessel are bonded together with clay.

Pressure Flaking: Chipping technique in which little spalls are removed by pressure, usually by a bone or antler tool.

Projectile Point: Pointed tip, usually of chipped stone, for any projectile weapon such as a spear, dart, or arrow.

Puna: High plateau of the Andes.

Quern: Milling stone.

Quipu: Knotted string device used by the Incas for recording numbers.

Radiocarbon: Carbon 14.

Resist Negative Painting: Technique of decorating pottery by covering the design area with liquid clay, applying an organic material to the background, and scorching the vessel to blacken the background while leaving the design in the original light color of the fired vessel.

Repoussé: Technique of decorating metal in which the piece is hammered over a carved mold.

Rocker Mill: Grinding device consisting of a large flat nether stone and a crescentic upper stone which is rocked back and forth on its curved edge.

Scraper: Chipped stone tool with a smooth, steep edge, used for preparing skins.

Spearthrower: Device consisting of a stick with finger grip and hook which serves as an extension of the arm and gives greater force in hurling a spear.

Specialization: Presence, in a society, of persons with full-time professions other than food getting.

Stirrup Spout: Pouring arrangement consisting of a hollow loop of clay both ends of which are attached to a bottle, with an open spout protruding from the top of the loop.

Stratigraphy: Layering of rocks, soil, refuse, etc., the deepest layer being the oldest and the uppermost the most recent.

Style: Formal characteristics of art or manufactured goods, in general or typical of a particular cultural complex.

Swidden: System of shifting cultivation typical of the tropical forest, characterized by slash-and-burn clearing of fields, planting without turning the soil, and very long fallow periods.

Synchoritic: (A settlement) having a dependent rural population.

Tapestry: Cloth made with independent wefts for each color area of the design.

Tenon Head: Carved stone head with a projection to be inserted into a wall.

Tie-dye: Technique of decorating textiles in which parts of the cloth are tied off to protect them from the dye, giving a design in natural color with a dyed background.

Twining: Technique of manufacturing textiles in which paired wefts, usually widely spaced, are intertwined between the warps.

Warp: In weaving, stationary yarns stretched between the two ends of the loom.

Wattle-and-daub: Construction technique consisting of canes or poles chinked with clay.

Weft: In weaving, transverse yarns passed back and forth across the warps.

Index